DAMES AND DAUGHTERS
OF THE FRENCH COURT

DAMES AND DAUGHTERS
OF THE FRENCH COURT
By Geraldine Brooks

Essay Index Reprint Series

BOOKS FOR LIBRARIES PRESS
FREEPORT, NEW YORK

First Published 1904
Reprinted 1968

PREFACE.

MUCH has been written about French women. Innumerable volumes pay homage to them as "Salonists," "Queens of Society," "Celebrated Women." One might almost say that there is no end to the literature that treats of these certainly very charming subjects. Here and there a writer, notably Sainte Beuve, has told of them so appreciatively, so ultimately, that to speak after such authority seems almost an impertinence.

However, it is sometimes pleasant to meet old friends in a new guise, even though the new guise be ever so simple and unpretentious. It is with this thought in mind that I venture to offer these "Dames and Daughters of the French Court."

It may seem that there is an incongruity in the title. Perhaps it is not as dames and daughters, those terms of eminently domestic flavor, that one naturally thinks of French women. Nevertheless, in spite of their salons, their social triumphs, and their literary and artistic successes, these French women really were dames and daughters as we understand the words. Apart from that very worldly world of which they were so conspicuous a part, they lived interior lives and experienced fireside joys and sorrows.

In my choice of characters I have remembered this. I have selected from the brilliant galaxy of French women the natural, the attractive, the lovable ones, those who seem most truly the dames and daughters of their country. They are preëminently worthy of an intimate acquaintance, of friendship, of affection. One cannot meet them too often. It is with this recommendation that I present them.

G. B.

NEW YORK, June, 1904.

CONTENTS

ILLUSTRATIONS

DAMES AND DAUGHTERS OF THE FRENCH COURT.

MADAME DE SEVIGNÉ.

Born at Bourbilly, Feb. 5, 1626.
Died at Grignan, April 18, 1696.

" It is impossible to speak of women without first putting one's self into a good humor by the thought of Madame de Sevigné." — *Sainte Beuve.*

FROM her Breton home, before ever she had visited Provence and Grignan Castle, Madame de Sevigné wrote to her daughter, the lady of the castle, " I have become quite at home in Grignan Castle. I see your rooms, I walk on your terrace, I go to mass in your beautiful church."

This is not mere talk on the part of Madame de Sevigné. She really was at Grignan, seeing its rooms, walking on its terrace, going to mass in its beautiful church. Her imagination, more swift in its flight than hippogrif or Pegasus, had in a twinkling carried her there.

It is for us who come after Madame de Sevigné
to make ourselves at home at "The Rochers,"
madame's Breton castle, even as madame made herself at home at Grignan, to take the journey thither
on wings such as madame employed — the wings of
imagination.

The old moss-grown chateau, breathing that air
of freshness, tranquillity, and simple grandeur which
characterized it in the time of Madame de Sevigné,
is waiting for us; the park with its long, shady
avenues is also waiting; and the garden sweet
with jasmine and orange flowers. The chapel door
stands open, and madame herself, blonde, smiling,
animated, is dallying on the slope of some sunny
terrace, chatting with her boon companion, Pilois,
the gardener.

Near by under the shade of the beech trees two
abbés are seated, the one a thrifty gentleman engaged with counters and accounts, the other,
younger than the first, an easy-going, visionary soul,
who leans back in his arm-chair with hands clasped
behind his head, dreaming idly.

There comes upon these two staid abbés an inter-
ruption in the pleasing form of a small, debonair,
young gentleman, dandling on silken hose and red-
heeled slippers, a bundle of books beneath his arm.
He talks a moment with the abbés, and the one
looks up from his accounts and the other stops his
dreaming to laugh at some tale which the young
man is telling.

Quickly, however, the young man turns from the abbés and leaves the shade of the beech trees for the sunshine of the terrace.

"Mother, mother beautiful," he calls, "will you not join us? We are all impatient for the reading and for you."

"Yes, yes, my little son, in a moment," she answers. Yet she tarries longer than a moment in further converse with the gardener.

Madame's "little son," who is in truth no less a personage than the Baron de Sevigné, looks from his mother to the abbés, makes a motion of comic resignation, and returns to the shade of the beech trees.

There Madame the Marquise, bright-eyed and breathless, at length joins the abbés and her son. She is eloquent in the narration of her news. Her little trees are growing surprisingly, she says; Pilois and she are raising their stately heads to the clouds; Pilois and she are planning to form new avenues; Pilois and she —

She can go no further. Saucily, jestingly, the young baron interrupts her, "Enough of Pilois. I grow jealous of Pilois," he declares. "He absorbs all your time, all your thoughts. I think you would rather listen to his tales than to any of Molier's or La Fontaine's that I may read you."

Madame the Marquise laughs gaily, "Pilois is a good fellow," she returns. "'T is true I enjoy his company and prefer his conversation to that of

many who have the title of chevalier in the parlia-
ment of Rennes.   Indeed, I am a worshipper of his
as you, my son, are a worshipper of the fair Ninon,
or our mouse here " — designating the younger
abbé with a motion of her hand — " of some heav-
enly vision, or the good uncle " — with an arch
smile for the elder abbé — " of the bright eyes of
his cash-box.   We must all have our idols," and
she shrugs her shoulders.

The young baron and the mouse (La Mousse
his name is) laugh at madame's sly raillery, but
the older man, madame's beloved " bien bon,"
regards his niece with a look more grave than
merry.

" We all know that another idol than Pilois
reigns in our lady's heart," he observes.

At this madame grows of a sudden very sad.
Her eyes fill with tears.   She raises her hand to
enjoin silence.

" You mean my daughter," she says.   " Let us
not speak of her."

For a moment there is silence.   Then it is observed that Marie, madame's French maid, is approaching.   She has crossed the court-yard and is
descending the sunny slope of the terrace.   Under
her arm she carries a small, silken-haired dog and in
her hand an embroidery frame.

She draws near and seats herself at the feet of
her mistress.   Madame takes from her the embroidery frame and begins working on a rare bit of

tapestry which, she explains, is to serve as altar cloth in her new chapel.

Marie, a pretty piece of human bric-à-brac, frilled, capped, and aproned according to the most approved code of Parisian maid servants, busies herself with the combing of Fidele's, the small dog's, silken coat. The young baron leans forward and pulls Fidele's tail, and rubs his nose and flicks his ears, alternately teasing and caressing him.

" Dost know thou art a usurper? " he inquires, playfully, of the dog. " Yes, sir, a usurper in the affections of your mistress. I might tell thee of another dog whom this faithless lady hath left behind her in Paris and to whom she hath solemnly vowed that she will love no other dog but him. And now she hath forgotten him for thee. I shall write and tell him of her fickleness and bid him go get himself a new and a more loyal mistress."

" Nay, my son, do not write Maphise, I entreat you," pleads madame. " He will think me a coquette, and I mean not to be a coquette, only Fidele hath besieged me with such sweet charms that I can no longer resist him. Scold me no more, dear son. Read to me instead. See, I am waiting and the abbés, they too, are waiting, and Marie and Fidele. We are all eager to be amused as you only can amuse us."

Thus implored, the young baron displays his books. One sees upon the covers such imposing

names as Tasso and Rabelais, Corneille and Tacitus,
and most conspicuous of all, Molier.

"Which shall it be?" he inquires. "The
audience shall be the choosers."

The abbés put in a vote for Tacitus and Marie's
glance favors Rabelais. But the marquise shakes
her head in dissent to all.

"The genius of our young baron is best suited
to Molier," she says. "He acts Molier so excel-
lently that one might easily mistake him for the
poet himself. Give us Tartuffe, my son, Tartuffe
to the life."

Thereupon, the shady spot beneath the beech
trees becomes a playground, and the young baron
an actor, and an enthusiastic audience laughs and
applauds.

It is thus that "The Rochers" is waiting for us.
Those whose flights of fancy can carry them where
they please should surely go thither. They will
find themselves in an atmosphere of perennial
pleasantness and cheer.

For those who take this journey to "The Rochers" an entertaining guide is to be had in
the letters of Madame de Sevigné. Of this
guide, of these letters, a great deal has been said.
Indeed, they have been as much praised as
any of the classics of French literature. And
one does not wonder that this should be so,
when one discovers their immortal freshness and
vivacity.

Of all the interesting things in the correspondence of Madame de Sevigné, and there are many, the most interesting is the woman herself. The smiling, witty, loving marquise charms us as she charmed the France of Louis Fourteenth. We want to know all that there is to know about her. We wish to make her our friend.

We learn that this Madame de Sevigné had something of a history, a history that was both gay and sorrowful. She came of an ancient Burgundian family. Fierce, " fire-eating " barons were her ancestors. A fund of moss-grown glory and tradition was her heritage.

She was born Marie de Rabutin-Chantal. Left early an orphan, she was brought up by her maternal uncle, the beloved " bien bon " whom we have seen living so pleasantly with her at "The Rochers," her livelong friend and companion, the Abbé de Coulanges.

The abbé's home was at Livry, a charming spot within driving distance of Paris. Here, in a romantic old abbey, in the shadow of a great wood, with the priest, her uncle, for guardian, amid the scent of honeysuckle and the songs of nightingales, Marie's girlhood was passed ; here from such learned gentlemen as Ménage and Chapelain she received her education, reading Spanish, Italian, and Latin, not in translation, but, as she herself expressed it, " in all the majesty of the original text;" and here, at length, brilliant, impudent, radiant, she bloomed into womanhood.

It must have been a real delight to behold Marie de Rabutin-Chantal, as she was then in all the freshness and sparkle of young womanhood, to catch the glint of her golden hair, the laughter of what she was pleased to term her " ill-matched eyes," and to note the lightnings of her ever changeful expression.

Her beauty, it has been said, was of a sort to defy the painter's art. It was a thing indefinite, illusive. Madame de La Fayette's verbal portraiture is the best likeness we have of her.

" The brilliancy of your wit," wrote Madame de La Fayette, " gives such lustre to your complexion and to your eyes that, although wit would seem to affect only the ears, it is nevertheless certain that yours dazzles the eyes. Those who listen to you no longer perceive that anything is wanting to the regularity of your features ; they concede you the most consummate beauty in the world."

Of course Marie had early her admirers, her lovers. First of all her tutor, Ménage, did his utmost to evolve, out of the relations of master and pupil, a romance. Marie laughed at him, teased him, and when he was angry won him back to good nature by all the most refined arts of coquetry. It was her plan, a plan to which she held constantly, to make all men her lovers and all women her friends.

Besides Ménage, one of Marie's girlhood lovers was her cousin, Bussy de Rabutin. Marie had much in common with this Bussy, wit, pride, and ancestry, and she used playfully to refer to the manifold tie that bound them by the happy term " Rabutinage."

It is a question whether or not the cousins ever came to any serious love-making. Bussy pretended to be frightened by the young Marie's "madcap" ways, as he called them, and declared tauntingly that she was "the prettiest woman in the world to be the wife of another." Certain it is that not Bussy, but a young nobleman, more bold and handsome and witty even than Bussy himself, finally married the "madcap."

The good uncle, who showed himself in all else so wise and practical a guardian, assuredly evinced a strange want of foresight in his choice of husband for his ward. But perhaps he could not help himself ; perhaps his charming blonde niece, whose heart was so passionately set on the new suitor, cajoled him into giving his assent.

From a worldly point of view, at least, the young Marquis de Sevigné was all that was deemed desirable. Wealth, rank, manly beauty, fine clothes, agreeable manners, were not lacking. Indeed, so well dressed were his vices that it is no great wonder they were mistaken for virtues by the trusting, generous, impetuous young woman to whom he addressed his proposals.

It was at two o'clock of a summer morning in
the year 1644, at the church of St. Gervais and St.
Portais in Paris that Marie de Rabutin-Chantal
was married to the Marquis de Sevigné. Despite
the earliness of the hour a long list of titled personages were present. They had come to wish
the young bride a joy that was destined to be very
brief.

The marquis carried his marquise off to his
ancestral home, "The Rochers." There they
remained for a long time, until their friends in the
city were forced to send them teasing madrigals to
lure them back to the world. This may be
supposed to have been a period of happiness for
the young wife.

The world to which Monsieur the Marquis and
Madame the Marquise at length returned was a
gay, jesting, infinitely social world. It was the
world of Voiture and Corneille, of Bossuet and
Ménage, a world that was making literature a
power and conversation an art. The Hotel de
Rambouillet over which Madame de Rambouillet,
the incomparable Athenice, as she was called,
reformer of morals, refiner of manners, presided
was at the height of its splendor. Here was to
be met a much admired, much respected company.

Walckenaer, Madame de Sevigné's biographer,
has given us a picture of one of the assemblages
at the Hotel de Rambouillet. He shows us the
ladies, bright with plumes and ribbons and gay

colors, smiling, listening, suave, gathered in the
stately, polished boudoir of the incomparable
Athenice, and ranged round them in bowing, com-
plimenting attendance the men—abbés, courtiers,
wits, writers, orators. Verses are read, criticisms
are passed, the merits and demerits of a certain
literary composition are minutely discussed.
Talent and good taste rule the day.

Such was the company, such the world which
welcomed the marquis and marquise back to
Paris. The young married pair had not been long
in the world when a secret concerning them was
whispered about. It was a tale of the young marquis's extravagance and infidelity. Madame,
whom every one admired, whom every one adored,
was neglected by her husband. He was a spendthrift and a libertine. "He loved everywhere,"
said Bussy, "but never anything so amiable as his
own wife."

The young marquis appears to have been quite
without shame. He coolly informed his young
wife that others might find her charming, but he
did not. Bussy the unscrupulous declared that to
madame's cold disposition her husband was
indebted for her loyalty. It seems that by some
evil-minded persons it had been supposed that
madame's resentment of her husband's faithlessness would make her an easy prey to their own
gallantries.

But the marquis and Bussy and those other evil-

minded persons did not know madame. Her good
sense and her high estimate of virtue were beyond
their comprehension. Her unworthy husband,
whom she could no longer respect, but whom to
her unhappiness she still continued to love, had
broken her heart. Her spirit of purity and integrity he had not broken. That was hers to keep
always.

It was at this period of bitterness and violated
love and confidence that a new experience came to
Madame de Sevigné. People have wondered why
she should have loved her daughter so passionately,
so beyond all reason. But when we consider that
she remembered neither father nor mother,
that she had no brothers or sisters, that
she had been deceived in her husband, that all
the tenderness and devotion of her affectionate nature, long repressed, was waiting for this daughter,
her passionate, unreasoning motherhood loses
something of its mystery.

Madame's daughter was born at Paris, and a year
later at "The Rochers" her son was born. Monsieur the Marquis appears to have regarded his
wife's presence as a reproach to his profligate behavior and to have kept her, therefore, at a distance
from him. Certain it is that while he was pur-
suing his wild course at Paris, she was living in
seclusion at "The Rochers," with her two children
and her uncle, the Abbé de Coulanges, and her
beautiful trees and alleys for companions.

When at length madame returned to Paris it was to face the most tragic event of her life. Shortly after her arrival her husband fought a duel for one of his mistresses and was killed by his rival. To lose her husband, whom, spite of his faithlessness, she loved, would have been of itself a blow, but to lose him in this humiliating way was indeed cruel. Whatever madame suffered, however, she suffered under a proud reserve. Yet that her anguish must have been keen we realize, when we learn that several years after, upon seeing D'Albert, the slayer of her husband, enter the room, she fainted.

Madame de Sevigné went back to "The Rochers," to the care of her children, to the guardianship of her uncle. There she lived quietly for several years, paying her husband's debts and lifting herself gradually out of that "abyss," as she expresses it, into which his fickleness and extravagance had plunged her. As for the man himself, so earnestly did she endeavor to forget him that never once did she mention his name to her children.

She was twenty-six years of age when, with fortune and spirit restored, she reëntered society. Mature in beauty, mature in wit, she was more charming even than in her girlhood days. She was enthusiastically received in all the fashionable salons of Paris. The Abbé Arnauld has given us a picture of madame as she then was.

" It seems to me," he says, "that I still see her
before my eyes as she appeared to me the first time
I ever had the honor of beholding her, when she
arrived, sitting in the depths of her great chariot,
that was thrown open wide.   On either side sat
the young gentleman, her son, and the young lady,
her daughter, all three such as those whom the
poets have described.   They recalled to me Latona
with the young Apollo and the young Diana, so
indescribable a charm radiated from all of them —
from the mother and the children."

Madame brought to the society into which she
had made so triumphant an entrance a happy,
laughing philosophy.   She regarded her frivolous
brothers and sisters, the reckless subjects of a reckless monarch, with charming leniency.   She did
not hold back her skirts when the faulty ones
approached.   She gave them her hand and smiled
indulgently upon them.   It was enough for her
that she kept her own self-respect and her own
good name.   She was not of the paste of which re-
formers are made.   She accepted the times as they
were and scattered about her an atmosphere of
flowers and sunshine.

Her friend Madame de La Fayette wrote of her,
" Your presence increases gaiety ; for joy is the true
element of your soul, and unhappiness more alien to
you than to any other person in the world."

It was supposed by the world in which madame
moved that, being of so social and agreeable a dis-

position, she would inevitably marry again. Many attempts were made to induce her to "change her condition." Conti, a prince of the blood, Turenne, a victorious general, Fouquet, a chancellor of the exchequer, were among her suitors. Yet, spite of the many sighs that were spent upon her, madame remained a widow. "I perceive every day," she told her daughter, "that the big fishes devour the small fry." Her love for her children, for her daughter especially, so filled her heart that there was left no room for any other affection.

To the tender passion, then, madame remained a stranger. But what she denied to love she gave warmly, generously, to friendship. Loyal, sincere, devoted, she satisfied, so La Rochefoucauld declared, "the ideas of friendship in all its conditions and consequences." Hers was the sort of friendship that adversity and ebbing fortune cannot change. To Fouquet at the time of his trial and to Pomponne after his fall from power she was an earnest and admiring partisan.

Madame herself used to wonder why she was so much beloved, why she was blessed with so many friends. The answer was in her own heart. She received only what she gave. The surest way to be loved, the wise man has told us, is to love.

So fond was madame of her friends, so dear was she to them, that she is incomplete without them. To know her we must know them.

Her children excepted, no one played so large a

part in her life as her cousin Bussy. We have
seen that he had been one of her earliest admirers and
that he and she were bound together by that pretty
tie of "Rabutinage." After her widowhood, Bussy
himself informs us, he was the first to speak to her
of love. He was at that time a widower and free.
He admits that he met with no success in his suit
and that, not being able to obtain his own way, he
was forced to content himself with loving her
after her own fashion. What that fashion was
we learn from his own words. "There is hardly
another woman in the kingdom," he remarked sig-
nificantly, "who can reduce her lovers to friends."

Bussy and madame were friends — warm, true
friends. But they had their falling out. Bussy,
it seems, was above all things vain and ambitious.
He wished for notoriety. To obtain this notoriety
he wrote a novel which he called "Amorous Cronicle of the Gauls " in which he satirized all the
most conspicuous men and women in society. His
book was very outrageous, but very amusing. It
won for itself many readers and for its author
many enemies. In consequence of it, Monsieur
Bussy was imprisoned in the Bastile for thirteen
months and then exiled to his Burgundian estates
for seventeen years. Notoriety he had obtained,
but at a severe sacrifice.

Madame, of course, was very angry when she saw
herself included in the "Amorous Cronicle." "If
horns had started from my head I could not have

been more amazed," she told him. " I read and
reread that cruel portrait. To find one's self in
print, the laughing stock of the Provinces, to be
on every book-shelf, in every one's hands; to
receive this cruel pain and from whom?"

Her " pain," her indignation, made Bussy very
repentant. He sought earnestly to repair the
injury that he had done. Let us read in his own
words the story of his expiation and of madame's
forgiveness. It happened at the time of the trial
of Fouquet, that former lover of madame, in whose
defence she was so eloquent and to whom she
referred as " our dear unfortunate."

" I shall never blame myself enough," wrote
Bussy, " for having offended the prettiest woman
in France, my near relative, whom I had always
loved and whose friendship I never had reason to
doubt. It is a stain on my life that I tried, indeed,
to obliterate when the surintendant (Fouquet) was
arrested, by loudly taking the part of the marquise
against those who had confounded her with the
mistresses of the minister. Not only generosity, but
truth, impelled me to act in this way. Before em-
barking on the marquise's defence I consulted
Tellier, who, except the king, alone had seen the
letters in Fouquet's casket. He told me that
those written by the marquise were the letters of a
friend of no little wit, and that they had delighted
the king far more than all the sentimental nullities
of the rest. The surintendant had been greatly

to blame when he mixed up friendship with so
much lovemaking. The marquise was much
pleased by my defence. Her kind heart and her
near relationship both caused her to forgive me and
since that time (which also was that of my disgrace) her affection for me rekindled; and except
for some explanations and some little reproaches
which a painful remembrance drew from her, there
are no marks of friendship which I have not
received from her since then, nor of gratitude that
I have not tried to show and that I shall not owe
her for the rest of my life. We resumed our
friendship in the first year of my exile."

Bussy was disappointed in his hopes, exiled, and
disgraced. In his loneliness madame's letters,
sparkling with wit, glowing with loyal, generous
friendship, must have been one of his chief comforts.

Of madame's friends surely there was no one so
important, so conspicuous as Bussy. But she had
other friends whom she loved more dearly and with
whom she was more intimate and more free spoken.
Chief among these were Madame de La Fayette
and the Duke La Rochefoucauld, and Monsieur
and Madame de Coulanges.

There could be no greater contrast than that
which existed between these two pairs of friends
of Madame de Sevigné. Madame La Fayette and
the duke, delicate in health, weary of the world,
lived a quiet, reflective life. She wrote her

romances and he his maxims. Each was devoted
to the other; both were thoughtful, serious, grave.
Monsieur and Madame de Coulanges were the
other extreme. They were all life and wit and
animation. They had no love for each other, only
a calm, forbearing consideration. They were
always in society, always laughing, always chatting, scattering epigrams, clever sayings, and
repartees wherever they went. Truly it was a
triumph for Madame de Sevigné to have won the
love of people of such different natures as these
two pairs of friends. It was a proof of the
breadth and versatility of her own soul.

Madame's friends were very near and dear to
her — they formed a large part of her existence.
But her children, more especially her daughter,
were her life, as necessary to her as the air she
breathed.

It has been said that madame's gifts of mind
were divided and distributed between her children.
The son was charming, but lacked stability. The
daughter had intellect, but " there was a heaviness
about her."

Of the two, the son appears to have been the
more lovable. We are inclined to quarrel a little
with the mother for preferring the daughter to
him. Since she was so unjust as to have a favorite
child, why was she not more reasonable in her
injustice, we inquire. Why did she not choose
her son? He was agreeable, winning, affectionate,

a most unselfish son and brother. He was a little
wild, to be sure. But his faults were of the time,
rather than of his own inclination. And then he
was such a charming penitent, was so good natured
and humble and witty under admonishment. We
are not at all surprised to hear that his mother's
scoldings of him generally ended in a burst of
laughter.

Nevertheless, it was not her amiable son, but her
phlegmatic daughter, whom madame loved best.
It is difficult for us to like this daughter. She
was so uncommunicative, so lukewarm, so calmly
philosophical, so very different from her mother.
When madame spoke or wrote she "opened the
flood gates." Her thoughts and her feelings
rushed forth impetuously for expression. Mademoiselle was timid, diffident, haughty, far removed
from her mother's tolerance and sweet self-forget-
fulness. Bussy said of the young lady, " This
woman has wit, but a tart wit, alloyed with intolerable vanity. She will make as many enemies as
her mother has made friends and adorers."

Spite of mademoiselle's asperity and pride, however, she was her mother's darling. Madame's
love for her daughter was a passion, a religion.
Arnault d'Audilly called the mother "a pretty
pagan." Madame herself said of her love, " It is
a constant devotion. It is what one ought to
render to God."

In the world in which madame lived, a frivolous,

volatile world that made passions of whims, whims
of passions, this sweet, tender, overwhelming mother-
love was regarded as an anomaly. People could
hardly believe it genuine. They spent much time
discussing it, wondering about it. At length
Monsieur de Pomponne solved the riddle of it.
There was played at court a game which was
called " Le Revers de la Medaille," the reverse
side of the cards. It consisted in guessing at the
realities that lie beneath the semblances. "Madame
de Sevigné *seems* to love her daughter passionately,"
he said. " Do you want to know what is on the
face of the card? Shall I tell you? Why this —
She loves her passionately."

Of madame's praises of her daughter we grow
a trifle weary. It is somewhat of a task to have
to agree with compliments with which we are
expected to agree. But for the great mother-love
we are all sympathy. It is something that appeals
deeply, keenly, to every one of us who has ever
loved.

Madame's love for her daughter was the ground
on which she took her stand in the world. To
bring out this daughter, to see her shine, was
madame's one desire. Mademoiselle de Sevigné
was very beautiful. She was of a more regular,
colder type than her mother. She danced admir-
ably and figured in the royal ballet with the charming young duchess of Orleans (whose tragic fate
Madame de La Fayette has touchingly recorded);

with Mademoiselle de Saint-Simon (the fair sister of the court historian) ; with the lovely Louise de la Vallière (that sweet sinner and penitent) ; and with Mademoiselle de Mortemar (who soon after became Madame de Montespan, the Cleopatra of King Louis's reign).

Racine, Boileau, and Fontaine, we are told, composed many madrigals in honor of Mademoiselle de Sevigné. She was hailed nymph and shepherdess and, in echo of her mother, "the prettiest girl in France." At length, in 1669, Monsieur de Grignan won her in marriage and bore her off to Provence, where in great state he ruled as governor of the province.

With the departure of Madame de Grignan to Provence dates the period of our intimate acquaintance with Madame de Sevigné. The adoring mother is separated from her darling. She is lonely and sad. Her one consolation is in writing to this daughter, in pouring out her heart on paper. Her letters become " torrents," she says, torrents that she cannot "keep back." Previous to this date madame has written letters to Bussy and to other of her friends. These letters have shown her to be a woman of wit and taste and feeling. But now in this correspondence with her daughter we are to find the spark of genius. Madame now writes without restraint, without traditional method. Her own fancy is her guide. Her thoughts and feelings flow impulsively, intuitively. She

scatters colors, images, impressions. " Her pen,"
as she expresses it, "has always the reins on its
neck." The secret is a soul has entered into her
correspondence, the soul of a profound, yearning
mother-love. It is the spring from which her
talent gushes forth ever fresh, clear, and sparkling.

It is thus she writes after the first cruel parting,
"Every thought stabs me with grief. Nothing
distracts me. I am always with you. I see the
coach always advancing, but never approaching. I
am always on the highroad, and sometimes feel
almost afraid lest the coach upset. I have a map
before my eyes and know every place where you
stop over night. Do write me about your trip by
boat. Alas ! how dear and precious to me is that
little vehicle the Rhone hurries so cruelly from me !
Ah, my dear, how I long just to see you, to hear
you, to embrace you, merely to see you pass by, if
the rest is too much to ask. . . . Unable
to keep back my thoughts of you, I have
begun to write to you, seated at the end of that little
shady walk you love, on the mossy seat where I
have seen you lying. But, Heavens ! where have
I not seen you here ! And how all these thoughts
pierce my heart ! I see you ; you are present to
me. I think and think again of it all. My wits
are in a whirl. But in vain I turn about, in vain
I search ; the dear child I love so passionately is
two hundred leagues away."

It was for the entertainment of " the dear child "

that madame composed her letters. To amuse this far-away daughter she related bits of gossip, humorous stories, pictured the gay tinsel existence at Versailles and the quiet, retired life at " The Rochers," told of the books she was reading, the thoughts she was thinking. Her letters are talks. They embody in perfection the spirit of French literature which was a genius for society and conversation. Very amusing are letters such as those which announce the engagement of the romantic Grande Mademoiselle to a man without fortune, rank, or worth, the dismissal of madame's faithful servant Picard, who refused to make hay, a piece of absence of mind on the part of Brancas, the most absent-minded of men, and a trick played by the king upon his devoted old courtier the Maréchal de Grammont. And very affecting are those letters of another sort which describe the sorrow of the Maréchal upon the death of his son, and of the Duchess de Longueville upon the death of her son, and despair of Vatel, the prince's cook, who killed himself in shame because the fish that were expected did not arrive on time. And very eloquent are the letters written upon the deaths of Turenne and Luvoise. All of these letters glow and pulsate with life. They transport us to Paris and Versailles, make us contemporaries of the Grand Monarch and his subjects, sharers of their joys and sorrows.

It is of the court and its people, of the gossip and stories told about them, that madame's correspondence has principally to do. But though she was primarily a painter of society she could represent nature as well.

Madame was of an adaptable disposition, as much at home in the woods and meadows of "The Rochers" as in any Parisian salon. She wrote of spending the afternoon in the fields "conversing with the cows and sheep." She knew the birds intimately, and corrected her daughter's superficial acquaintance with them. "Where do you find that nightingales are heard on the thirteenth of June? Ah, they are too busy then caring for their little households. They no longer think of singing or of making love; they have more serious business." She mourned the felling of a tree as the loss of a friend. When her son caused a portion of the ancestral woods to be cut down in order to raise money to meet some foolish expenses, she was greatly grieved and wrote plaintively of the outcast crows and owls, wood gods and dryads, who made complaints to her and touched her very heart. With infinite skill she celebrates "the triumph of the month of May when the nightingale, the cuckoo, and the linnet open the springtime in our forests." She makes us enjoy with her "those fine, crystalline days of autumn which are no longer warm and yet not cold." And she does not neglect winter, but appreciatively relates its charms when the trees are adorned with pearls and crystals. She observed the various stages of spring so carefully, the gradual transitions and shadings of the leaves on hornbeams, beech, and oak trees, as they passed from red to green that she at length declared, "At a pinch I don't know but that I could make a spring myself."

Madame had a genius for society, and an intelligent love of nature. She possessed also energy and originality of mind. She was not carried away by the excesses of the time. In politics she showed a degree of independence. She admired the king, but believed him human, and saw the folly of undue flattery of him. " I am told," she writes, " that the Minin monks in dedicating a thesis to the king have compared him to God, but in such a way as to make it plain that God is but a copy. Too much, too much." And again, " What will courtiers not do to please their masters ? " she demands. " Do they reckon health, pleasure, property, life itself, of any moment compared with obeying and pleasing him ? If such were our feelings toward God what saints we would be ! "

In religion she was not wholly pious like her friends at Port Royal, nor altogether frivolous like her acquaintances at court. She had both worldliness and other-worldliness. She was the means between the two extremes. Her belief was in a providential fatalism. " To my mind," she writes, " the author of the universe must be the cause of all that happens. When I must needs

blame Him I blame no one and submit. It was de-
creed that there should be a Madame de Sevigné loving her daughter more than any other mother loves
hers, that she should be separated from this
daughter, and that the keenest sufferings she
should experience in life should be occasioned by
this dear child." And in the same vein, referring to
the death of Monsieur de Turenne, she says : " For
myself, who see Providence in all things, I see that
cannon loaded from all eternity. I see everything
leading Monsieur de Turenne to its mouth, and I
find nothing hurtful in all this, supposing his conscience to be in good condition. What would he
have? He dies in his glory ; his reputation could
gain nothing more. In that moment he enjoyed
the satisfaction of seeing his enemies retreat — of
reaping the fruit of his three months' endeavors.
Sometimes in the course of a long life the star
grows dim."

On the mystery of life and death she passed many
grave reflections. "As for my life, you know it,"
she declares. " I spend it with five or six friends
whose society is pleasant to me, and in the per-
formance of a thousand necessary duties — no light
affair. But what troubles me is that nothing is accomplished day by day, and life is made up of days,
and we grow old and we die. This, I think, is
very sad." And again, " Alas, how death goes up
and down, striking on every side ! " she exclaims.
" I find myself bound by an awkward engage-

ment. Launched into life without my consent, I
must leave it; this overwhelms me. And how
shall I leave it? Whither? By what door?
When will it be? With what preparation? How
shall I stand with God? What shall I have to
offer him? What can I hope for? Am I worthy
of heaven? Do I deserve hell? What an alter-
native! What a perplexity! I might better have
died in the arms of my nurse."

There are no wiser, pleasanter reflections upon
old age than hers. " Providence," she writes, " leads
us with so much goodness through the different
stages of our life that we hardly are conscious as
they pass by. The change is effected with such
gentleness that it is imperceptible. It is the hand
on the dial, which we do not see moving. If at
twenty they were to show us in a looking-glass
the countenance which we have or should have at
sixty, comparing it with that of twenty, we should
be quite overcome and horrified at that face; but it
is unnoticeably that we grow older. To-day we
are as we were yesterday, and to-morrow as to-day;
and thus we go on without feeling the change, and
this is one of the miracles of that Providence that I
adore." And in continuation of this same theme,
" You know," she says, " that I never could endure that old people should say, ' I am too old to
correct myself.' I could more easily forgive the
young folks in saying, ' We are too young.' Youth
is so attractive that we could only adore it if the

soul and the mind were as perfect as the body ;
but when one is no longer young, then it is that one
must try to perfect one's self and try to make up in
good qualities what one has lost in the agreeable
ones. For this reason, every day I mean to im-
prove in soul, in mind, in sentiment."

Reverie played a large part in Madame de
Sevigné's life. And so, too, did reading. She was
always, as she herself declared, "a devourer of
books." She read everything from Rabelais, who
made her "die of laughing," to Nicole who made
her "quake with fear." She was desirous that
her grandson should develop a taste for reading,
and lamented that his young blood made "such a
din " that he did not hear her wishes. And
when she learned that Pauline, her granddaughter,
was fond of books she was delighted. "She is
beyond the reach of tedium and idleness, two hor-
rid pests," she wrote.

We would expect of a woman like madame, one
who thought so deeply and so broadly and who
read so widely, that she would rise above the pre-
judices of her time. Therefore we are shocked at
the lightness with which she describes the sufferings of the poor peasants of Brittany who, driven
by the tyranny of their duke to rebel against him,
are conquered by armed force and cruel executions.
We are disturbed, too, by the weakness of the re-
monstrance that escapes her when she learns that
her little granddaughter D'Adhémar is to be sacri-

ficed, immured for life with all her pretty hopes
and passions in a convent. We look for a genuine
protest, a righteous indignation on the part of the
kind-hearted marquise. But we are disappointed.
Madame's fault was a too easy acceptance of
the wrongs of the times. She who was so sweet,
so charming, so sensible, was not perfect. We
regret the little that was lacking to make her
ideal and mourn her failing as that of a dear
friend.

Madame was over-indulgent. Yet she could
resent, she could denounce. And, when at length
her voice is raised in censure, it rings very true
and clear and forceful. Madame was not in sympathy with the extravagance of the age in which she
lived. She was not of the class which believed
that to keep a strict account of expenses was
beneath one's dignity and honor. In her economies
madame was a plebian. She declared vehemently
against the reckless living of her daughter and
son-in-law. She accused them of being "two
spendthrifts, the one demanding, the other approv-
ing everything." She complained bitterly of the
"cruel and continual cheer of Grignan" and
prophesied that the fabric of which their glory
was constructed would prove illusive and dissolve
at a touch.

The Grignans, however, gave no heed to her
words of wise protest. Their castle remained "an
inn" where eighty to a hundred guests were con-

stantly entertained and where the gaming table
forever made and unmade fortunes.

Madame's daughter and son-in-law were but
living the life of the rest of the aristocracy of the
day. The whole court was on the brink of bank-
ruptcy. In vain daughters were cloistered and the
portions of the younger sons appropriated. The
nobility was without money, without resources.
Their only refuge was the bounty of the king.
Like Bussy they "embraced his knees" in the
hope that finally they might "reach his purse."
In the words of Madame de Sevigné, they "paid
court to him" on the chance that "some drop-
pings might fall upon them."

Madame, of course, despite her disapproval,
helped the Grignans generously. She gave also
to her son, for whom a commission in the army
must be purchased and those luxuries furnished
which were incumbent on his state. On her
children's account madame was near to ruin. But
her own thrift and the ability of the good uncle,
who was her steward, preserved her. She retired
to "The Rochers" and lived there sparingly.
savingly. At length by slow degrees her fortune
was reinstated.

Meanwhile the young, radiant Latona, whom
we saw riding with her two beautiful children in a
coach drawn by prancing horses, was gone. In
her place there had come a stately, white-haired,
frugal lady. There may have been wrinkles on

this lady's countenance. There were none in her
heart. She was as charming, kind, and generous
as that Latona had been.

Her house in Paris, the Hotel Carnavalet, where
for so many years she had entertained and had
written her immortal letters, was closed. Madame's
last years were spent amidst the tranquil, serene
beauty of "The Rochers." Her son, always sweet
tempered and genial, a better son, perhaps, than
madame deserved, since she so infinitely preferred
her daughter, was with her. By now he was "a
gray-bearded ensign" and had brought with him
to "The Rochers" a delicate, fragile little wife of
whom the elder marquise came to be very fond.

At length our Madame de Sevigné looked for the
last time, not knowing it, upon her beloved trees
and walks and terraces, and the moss-grown
chateau in which so much of her life had been
passed. She left the rugged north behind her and
descended into the sunshine of the south, a sunshine that was the more glowing because of the
dear daughter who dwelt therein. Let us leave
her at her journey's end, smiling and contented,
amid the olives and orange groves, with her daughter's hand in hers.

MADAME DE LA FAYETTE.

Born in Paris in March, 1634.
Died in Paris on May 25, 1693.

"The most intellectual woman and the best female writer in France." — *Boileau.*

OPPOSITE the Petit Luxembourg in the Rue de Vaugirard stood the home of Madame de La Fayette. It was a fine house with a pleasant garden attached. Many were the illustrious persons, weary of the frivolities of court and with a taste for letters and serious conversation, who repaired thither. It was a relief, they said, to escape from the whirlpool a moment and to recover their breath and draw new life and inspiration in the serene atmosphere of madame's drawing-room.

Now it was Segrais, the poet wit, who presented himself; there was manuscript beneath his arm — he had come, like as not, to ask madame's opinion on a story of his or to help in the construction of a story of hers. And now it was La Fontaine; he had written, perhaps, some verses and wished to inscribe them to madame. Sometimes the Cardinal de Retz was a visitor, and sometimes the Prince de Condé. Madame de Maintenon, before the days of her elevation, was a near neighbor of Madame

33

de La Fayette and came often to see her; she had always some just and sage remark at her tongue's end. Madame de Coulanges came, too, and no one in all the little coterie was so vivacious, so volatile as she. But the one who was most welcome and most loved, she of the sunny countenance, affectionate greeting, and witty story, was she whom we immediately recognize as Madame de Sevigné.

Madame de La Fayette, a tall, frail figure, sombrely and yet richly dressed, a pensive, gentle, calmly judicious presence, received her friends with that blending of candor and reserve which was her distinguishing trait. With her, at her side, there was always a certain notable gentleman. He was no longer young, and gout pinned him to a chair, but his face while sad and cynical was supremely noble. This gentleman was famed throughout France as the Duke de la Rochefoucauld.

The world, which was never known to spare anybody, had not spared Madame de La Fayette. It criticised her for many things. It declared that she was notional, that her many illnesses were imaginary rather than real. It had much to say in ridicule of the lace curtains with which she adorned her bed. But most of all it busied itself in gossip about her friendship with the Duke de la Rochefoucauld.

Was it friendship, or was it love, every one inquired. " The fear of the Lord on the part of

Marie Madeleine Piche de la Vergne.

DE LA FAYETTE.

Née en 1633. Morte en 1693.

Dequevauviller Sc.

MADAME DE LA FAYETTE.

From a portrait by B

both and perhaps also policy have clipped Cupid's wings," one reflective woman determined. The too suspicious Bussy shook his head: "I maintain that there is love between them," he asserted.

To this medley of opinion Madame de Sevigné hastened, eager to defend. She interposed words of earnest faith and admiration, spoke feelingly of the charm of their friendship, their " delicious communions," and their confidence in each other. " Such a tie," she concluded, " seems to me stronger than any passion."

Posterity has decided upon the intimacy between Madame de La Fayette and the duke, and has decided with Madame de Sevigné. This intimacy, every one now agrees, was friendship, an ideal friendship, legitimate, earnest, steadfast. It had all the tenderness, all the softness, all the warmth of love, and the calm, clear strength of an intellectual alliance. In truth, it was a romance, a romance without storms, wholesome and serene, and one quite befitting the life of so sweet and rational a woman as Madame de La Fayette.

It was a late romance. Madame, its heroine, was a mature, a sane, an eminently serious woman. She had almost forgotten the playtime of her early youth. But Madame de Sevigné, her friend, had not forgotten and delighted to recall it. " Despite her discretion, we laughed and had our frolics," she declared.

So it was, Madame de La Fayette had had her frolics. Before the days of her madameship, when she was known as Mlle. Marie Madeleine Pioche de la Vergne, she had been gay and girlish, but always in a very gentle way. "That old Mènage," she had called Mènage, her tutor, and he in turn had punned on her name and designated her "Laverna," which in Latin is to say "the thief." It was his heart that she had stolen. The amorous pedant made it a point to fall in love with the prettiest and brightest of his pupils — first with the witty, teasing, fair-haired Marie de Rabutin Chantal, and six years later with this other Marie who, if not so sparkling as her predecessor, was of a more poetic, delicate turn of mind. "Spirituelle," the Abbé Costar called her. "Tout lumineuse, tout precieuse," the poet Scarron said of her.

Of course she proved a brilliant scholar. Her father, who was field-marshal and governor of Havre, was proud of her and engaged the best masters to come and teach her. Mènage and Father Rapin together developed her young mind. She soon caught up with them in learning. One day when they were discussing as to the correct translation of a certain passage, she came forward, very modestly we may be sure, and said, "You are both wrong," and with that she herself read the passage as it should be read. The masters had to confess themselves vanquished, and by a girl. It was poetry, we are told, that she interpreted so glibly.

With Cicero she would have naught to do. Virgil
and Horace were her idols, and it was to them she
gave her thoughts. It was the poets whom she
loved and understood so perfectly.

Mademoiselle was learned, but she did not desire
to be so considered. She was well aware of the
ill favor that attaches to "blue stockings," and
she wisely avoided it. When questioned outside
the school-room as to the meaning of an iambus
she trippingly replied that it was the opposite of a
trochee. And no one, save her masters and her
friends, guessed at the wealth of knowledge which
her light manner hid.

Thus her school-days passed pleasantly. When
she was fifteen, however, her father died and her
mother, who, though a good woman, was frivolous
and gay, very soon married again. Mademoiselle's
step-father, to whom it has been stated she did not
take very kindly, was the Chevalier Renand de
Sevigné, uncle of that young Marquis de Sevigné
who had recently taken as wife the sunny, impulsive, light-hearted Mademoiselle de Rabutin Chantal. And so it was that these two women, destined
to play parts graceful and important in their
country's history, met for the first time.

Together Mademoiselle de la Vergne and the
young Marquise de Sevigné frequented the Hotel de
Rambouillet. They were to be seen there often
seated side by side. They were one in their
admiration of Corneille and in their dislike of all

that savored of the pedantic and affected. They
were not of those "Femmes Savantes," at whom
Molière afterwards aimed his darts. Their sense
of humor and their knowledge of the fitness of
things preserved them from ridicule. From the
Hotel de Rambouillet they took away with them
what was best of its spirit, and left behind all that
was false and foolish.

It was not long after her meeting with Madame
de Sevigné that Mademoiselle de la Vergne
became the wife of the Compte de La Fayette. Of
the Compte little is known. He appears to have
effaced himself almost completely. It is related of
him only that he married and died young, leaving
his wife with two sons and the name which she was
to render famous.

It is an interesting fact concerning madame's
husband that he was the brother of the beautiful
Louise de La Fayette whom Louis XIII. had
loved and whom the cloister held as Mère Angel-
ique. Madame de La Fayette went often to visit
her sister-in-law at the convent and there, for the
first time, she saw Princess Henrietta of England
and there her friendship with the princess began.
Later, when the princess married the brother of
the king of France and under the official title
"Madame" became a central figure in the court
circle, Madame de La Fayette was summoned to
her side. The princess was deeply attached to her
and could not get on without her; Madame de La

Fayette herself could not understand wherefore,
and finally decided that it could only be by chance
that she who was of so grave a nature should please
so young and frivolous a woman as *Madame.*

Madame lived a life of romantic adventure and
intrigue. She confided all her secrets to Madame
de La Fayette, and at her request Madame de La
Fayette confided them to paper. The result was a
charming book of Memoirs. Thanks to the gentle,
loving pen of the writer, the youthful indiscretions
and errors of the princess are softened and the
princess herself, who "knew not the meaning of the
word rancor," shines forth in the true light of
her sweet, winning, unselfish personality. The
little volume ends suddenly and sadly with a
death-bed scene. As we read, we seem to see the
author's tears staining the pages. *Madame* died in
Madame de La Fayette's arms. Her death was a
sorrow for which Madame de La Fayette never con-
soled herself. She said that it cast a shadow over
the rest of her life. On the third anniversary of
Madame's death she wrote to Madame de Sevigné,
" I reread some of her letters yesterday. My heart
is full of her."

During the years that Madame de La Fayette
moved at court Louis was at the height of his pros-
perity. She was surrounded by successful authors,
victorious generals, and a smiling, polished gallantry. She kept in the background, however, looking on rather than taking any active part. She

was withal something of a critic, and even ventured to write a satire on the fashionable jargon of the day. One fancies her a woman, still young and of an attractive personality, attending *Madame's* parties at Fontainebleau and St. Cloud, observing all that went on about her and making mental notes which were to stand her in good stead when she came to write the romances of her later years. She spoke seldom, but always to the point. Her word carried weight with it and even was regarded as a kind of ultimate authority.

When *Madame* died, Madame de La Fayette retired from court. She was sad for the loss of her friend and her health was beginning to fail. Moreover, her natural inclination was for society of a more serious and more literary caste. She occasionally frequented the salon of the Grande Mademoiselle and that of Madame de Sablé at Port Royal. She is represented as one of the inhabitants of the Chamber of the Sublime." She is pictured as seated beside Madame Thianges reading verses while Bossuet and the Duke de la Rochefoucauld, the Duke de Maine and Monsieur de Marsiallac in another part of the room read more verses, and Despereaux with a pickaxe holds at bay seven or eight bad poets and Racine, safely installed at his side, beckons to La Fontaine to join them. The poets of her own day to whom her tastes and talents were allied were appreciated in a measure by Madame de La Fayette. She was on friendly terms with Molière, Boileau, and La Fontaine. But ever faithful to the author of the "Cid," she retained for him her chief allegiance.

Madame de La Fayette herself began to write at an early date. She wrote merely for her own pleasure and because she could not help doing so. Authoresses were not in favor then. Women were told that they should inspire, but must not write. Madame, therefore, took into her literary confidence only a few of her most faithful and most indulgent friends. Segrais was at first her chief adviser. He helped her in the arrangement of her plots and in her methods of construction. He even lent his name to "Zayde," her first real work, which appeared at the close of 1670. People were easily deceived into believing him the author. The story closely resembled his work, still retaining much of the exaggerated, romanesque style. But here and there were touches, delicate, subtle, true to life, which gave promise of the dawning of a new star in the literary firmament and of the new era which this star was to introduce.

At the time of the publication of "Zayde," Madame de La Fayette and the Duke de La Rochefoucauld had for five years been united in that peculiar tie which bound them so happily and so indissolubly together, and which gave the world so much to talk about. Theirs was not one of those affections which Madame de La Fayette has somewhere defined as " the passions which

snatch us irresistibly from ourselves." Rather it
was the kind conscious of itself, slower and more
sure. When for the first time they met each other
in Madame de Sablé's salon, the duke was a man
fifty years old. He had passed through all manner
of romantic experiences and situations, yet had
never been, Madame de Sevigné tells us, what may
be truly called "a lover." "Love," he declared,
with his cold, cynical smile, "is nowhere but in
novels." He saw Madame de La Fayette. He
talked with her. She was, it is true, still young
in years, about thirty, but there was maturity and
womanly wisdom in her soul. He admired the
justice of her mind, the sincerity of her nature.
Segrais had praised her candor and had related as
an instance of it that she never concealed her age,
but told freely in what year she was born. La
Rochefoucauld, in his turn, admired that candor.
He said in praise of Madame de La Fayette that
she was "genuine." It was the word that best
described her. Madame de La Fayette, on her
part, we may imagine, was flattered when she perceived the impression she was making on so distinguished and important a man as the duke. She
divined too his noble nature. She saw that he was
something beyond the misanthrope, the author of
the "Maxims." She longed to sweeten his
thoughts, to lead his perverted nature back to its
original clear channels. Thus it was that their
friendship came about gradually and deliberately.

It was at first a matter of intellect, but at length heart entered in and it became that something delicate, romantic ideal which one finds so indefinable.

It is through the letters of Madame de Sevigné that we catch glimpses of the quiet monotony, the mutual sympathy of the daily lives of these two friends. It is true that the pervading atmosphere of their existence is one of cloud rather than of sunshine. The duke is crippled with his gout and madame's fever is constantly overtaking her. " We have conversations so sad," says Madame de Sevigné, " that it seems as if there was nothing to do but to bury us." But the garden close at hand is full of the sweetest perfumes. Sometimes, when health and spirits are at their best, the dining-hall is merry with guests. Now and then, even, there is a jaunt to the opera, and Lulli's " Cadmus " moves not only the impulsive Madame de Sevigné, but even the reserved Madame de La Fayette to tears. Another time it is the " Poetique " of Despereaux that snatches them from themselves. We even find mention of a sojourn to the court where Madame de La Fayette with some other ladies drives in the king's calash and is shown the sights of Versailles and delights his majesty with her judicious praise.

All this, however, is but the occasional. There are other times, unfortunately more frequent, when Madame de La Fayette is too ill to see her friends. She is utterly weary, tired even of saying " good

morning " and "good evening." Then she escapes
to the country, and Madame de Sevigné, in her
absence, finds a deserted garden and a duke
incredibly sad. The flowers still bloom; they
have the sunshine and the fresh air to cheer them.
But the "friend of her soul" can find no comfort
in a life from which she has departed.

Gourville, the servant of the duke, was jealous
of Madame de La Fayette and used to say that she
had taken entire possession of his master. Madame
de La Fayette had a gentle but commanding way
and it may be that Gourville was right. It was a
willing, a happy and beneficial thraldom, however.
One scarcely recognizes in the friend of Madame
de La Fayette the cynical author of the "Maxims."
Madame de Sevigné tells us of his "soul unsurpassed
for fortitude, wisdom, kindness, and strength," and
says that he is a patriarch and knows almost as
well as herself "a mother's tenderness." He sends
pretty little compliments to her daughter. He is
kinder in his manner, less bitter in his speech. One
detects the influence of Madame de La Fayette.
Where there was once a belief in universal corruption there is now forbearance, even a mild hopefulness. That was true which Madame de La Fayette
herself said: "He stimulated my intellect, but I
reformed his heart."

Together madame and the duke, alike ill and
sad, talked and wrote and received their friends.
Moreover, madame, who numbered among her ac-

complishments an understanding of jurisprudence, managed the affairs of the duke and restored his fallen fortunes. Then, too, being a close friend of the Duchess of Savoy, madame acted as a sort of secret agent for the duchess. Her parlor became, for the affairs of Savoy, something like a private bureau. Madame heard everything, saw everything, advised and planned and managed, was indeed the skilled and helpful diplomat to perfection.

In the midst of a life so full, so occupied, Madame de La Fayette found little time for the letter writing which she hated. "If I had a lover who wished to hear from me every day," she said, "I should break with him." Her poor correspondence was the one complaint which Madame de Sevigné raised against her. We know the protesting letters of the impetuous marquise. To them Madame de La Fayette at length replied in a tone gentle and soothingly affectionate: "Now, my dear, why are you screaming like an eagle? Do not measure our friendship by our letters. I shall love you as much in writing only a page in a month as you in writing ten in eight days."

This was true, and Madame de Sevigné knew that it was. Indeed she had never really doubted Madame de La Fayette. The two understood each other perfectly. "There was never," Madame de Sevigné herself declared, "the slightest cloud on our friendship."

The same could not be said of Madame de La
Fayette's friendship with Madame de Maintenon.
Here bitterness crept in and a close attachment of
many years ended in disagreement and coolness.
Both were judicious, intellectual, and candid, both
hated pretension and admired simplicity and earnestness. They had much in common. Each
praised the other for her uniform bearing. And
yet it was this same simplicity, candor, and uniform bearing in Madame de La Fayette which, it
has been hinted, offended Madame de Maintenon
when she became the wife of the king of France.
Madame de Maintenon's ideas, it is to be feared,
changed with her condition. No doubt she desired
from Madame de La Fayette a greater consideration
because of her own acquired state. This, of course,
Madame de La Fayette, the straightforward, never
gave her. They went their different ways. Meanwhile it was not in the ante-chamber of Madame
de Maintenon that polite manners found their best
expression; there reform went too far, and austerity carried the day. Rather it was the salon of
Madame de La Fayette that saw the most satisfying
triumphs of society and conversation.

Madame de La Fayette maintained her uniform
bearing. She flattered no one. She wrote few
letters. She made few visits. Yet she won and
kept many friends. " No one," Madame de Sevigné
said, " accomplished so much without leaving her
place. She has a hundred arms," continued her

enthusiastic friend; "they reach everywhere."
What was the charm, one asks. It was of intrinsic
worth. Madame de La Fayette, to use La Rochefoucauld's word for her once more, was "genuine,"
and she was sane and just. People said of her
that her judgment was superior to her intelligence,
and it was the compliment that pleased her best.
She was quiet, almost languid in her manner. It
was a theory of hers that people should live without ambitions and without passions : " It is enough
simply to exist," she said. Yet, one was conscious
always of a reserve force, and of a delicate sensibility as well. She who was so calm, so reticent,
it is known, shed tears over Lulli's Cadmus, avoided
good-byes between herself and Madame de Sevigné
because of the pain they caused her, and at the
hint of any danger to the duke was instantly
alarmed and tearful. Thus it was that her character was one of strength and her feelings of tenderness ; and for both she was loved. Moreover, the
refinement of her thought as expressed in her
speech was an additional attraction. Her compari-
son of poor translators to the lacqueys who stupidly
bungle and distort the compliments with which
they have been entrusted by their mistresses is one
of the many true and striking remarks for which
madame was distinguished and which lingered long
afterwards in the memory of her listeners.

Such was Madame de La Fayette's charm, a serious rather than a gay one. And so it was felt to

be by her friends. While others were known as
" The Sunbeam," " The Rainbow," and " The Leaf,"
she was " The Mist." She lingered on the heights
and one could only faintly see the blue beyond and
the sunshine peeping through. The blue was always
pale, the sunshine veiled. Hers was not a nature
of brilliancy, light, and color, but of soft, subtle
shades. Yet there was a restfulness about her,
a peace and comfort which the more gaudy and
more dazzling ladies could not bestow. So thought
the duke.

It was when the friendship between Madame de
La Fayette and the duke was at its height that
" The Princess de Cleves " was written. Together
the two friends sat and dreamed and planned.
Madame wrote, and the duke, whose literary taste
was excellent, revised and approved. Thus employed, the hours passed pleasantly. The world of
fact, of sickness, age, and sad experience was forgotten. Together the two friends entered the realm
of youth and poetry and romance. In the heroine
Madame de la Fayette's own early, sweet imaginings
were pictured, and in Monsieur de Nemours the
duke saw himself as he had been in youth, only
idealized and uncontaminated by contact with the
baser elements of life. That mild, equable light
which arose from their own tranquil love suffused
the characters of their creation. The atmosphere of
the book was one of sentiment, true, pure, and
simple sentiment, touched with reality. The spirit

of their own happy, soul-communings had entered
in. As they approached the end, the tone grew grave
and sombre. The close was one of renunciation
and triumphant sacrifice. It was as if they felt
only too keenly the brevity of life and the nearness
of that inevitable separation which fate held in store
for them.

The book was completed and appeared in the
spring of 1678. Immediately the princess became
the person most talked of. Her name was on everybody's lips. People stopped one another in the
Tuileries to inquire about her. She was read and
read again, and yet again. And she was criticised
and she was dramatized. Indeed, she was quite the
event of the season.

The authorship of the book was veiled. Segrais,
the Duke de La Rochefoucauld, Madame de La Fayette, no one of them would acknowledge it. "The
book is an orphan," wrote Madame de Scudery, "dis-
owned both by father and mother." Madame de La
Fayette even went so far as to write critically and
quite impersonally of it. "As for myself, I am flattered at being suspected of it," she said. "I believe I
should acknowledge the book if I were assured that
the author would never appear to claim it. I find it
very agreeable and well-written without being
excessively polished, full of things of admirable
delicacy which should be read more than once; above
all, it seems to be a perfect presentation of the
world of the court and the manner of living there.

It is not romantic or ambitious; indeed it is not a romance; properly speaking it is a book of memoirs, and that I am told was its title, but it is changed. Voila, my judgment upon Madame de Cleves."

Proof is not wanting, however, to show that the book is the work of Madame de La Fayette "assisted by the taste" of Monsieur de La Rochefoucauld. It marked a new epoch in the novel. In place of the stilted and impossible, it substituted the easy and the natural. Adventures in it were few. The story depended for its interest on the analysis of character and of motive. It was narrated simply, delicately, quietly. One lingered over its pages in pensive, happy mood, even as the lovers of whom it told lingered along the banks of "the brook bordered by willows." Its characters were of the Court of Henry II., but they were very like the characters of the Court of Princess Henrietta, whom Madame de La Fayette had known and studied. There was present the same grace, the same gallantry and lightness, the same France. Its charm was its freshness, its purity, its truth, the qualities that live. And so, quite modestly, without flourish of trumpet or call to arms, it took its place among French classics.

The romance completed, the pen laid aside, Madame de La Fayette and the duke rested and watched the effect of the little volume. Its success was the closing happiness of a life together that had held much of happiness. For the last time the two friends read and conversed together and saw in each other's eyes that mutual understanding and tenderness that was so dear to both. Then the duke died.

"Madame de La Fayette has fallen from the clouds," wrote Madame de Sevigné. "There is comfort for all others, but none for her." In vain the poor lady sought to interest herself in new schemes, in the enlargement of her house. She found only that her loneliness increased. She tried to console herself with the friends that remained to her. But these had divided interests. Nowhere could she find that constant thought, that absolute affection which she had always received from the duke. She could not, as Madame de Sevigné declared, "so close up her ranks as to fill the vacant place." There was left only God and death.

Madame de La Fayette turned her thoughts to Heaven, not with the exaltation of a religieuse,— "divine reason" was still her guide,— but with resignation and hope. Her life had been quiet yet full, she thought. She had little to regret, much to be thankful for. And thus, with sweet sanity, patient and gentle to the end, she died.

MADAME GEOFFRIN.

Born in Paris, 1699.
Died in Paris, Oct. 6, 1777.

" Madame Geoffrin is an extraordinary woman with more common sense than I almost ever met with." — *Horace Walpole.*

SHE is a unique figure, this Madame Geoffrin. The memoirs of the seventeenth century 'show her to us an elderly, sensible, proper sort of person. We think that we are not going to like her, that we are going to find her stupid and commonplace. We end by discovering her to be a woman of remarkable power and charm, and by liking her as we would like an affectionate school-ma'am or an indulgent stepmother.

It is thus that the society of her time knew and admired her. The men and women who came to see her at her house in the Rue Saint-Honoré, who courted her patronage, who submitted themselves to her empire, were her boys and girls, her school-children, her sons and daughters. They called her mamma, and took her scoldings gracefully as obedient children should ; or, if they were not in the mood for scoldings, they ran away, played truant, yet returned inevitably to the maternal knee. They begged to be scolded again, having

MADAME GEOFFRIN.
From a painting by Staal.

found her frowns more necessary than the smiles of the rest of the world. They were attracted, too, by those sugar-plums which she bestowed at intervals, sugar-plums in the shape of life annuities. They were tied, so to speak, to her apron. She had them in leading strings.

It is as a mamma, a schoolmistress, a mature and motherly soul, that Madame Geoffrin seems to have made her first appearance in the world. One remembered her always with silvery hair, her cap tied under her chin, a bit of exquisite lace about her throat, and wearing soft, silky gowns of sombre shade. She never endeavored like some women, it is said, to appear younger than she was. She dressed not for "yesterday's age," but for "to-morrow's." This added to her natural air of dignity and quiet elegance.

There was, however, a prehistoric period of youth to which Madame Geoffrin's own mind occasionally reverted. She spoke of it briefly to her friends. She was of bourgeois birth, she said. Her father had been a *valet de chambre.* She could remember neither father nor mother. Her grandmother, a sensible old lady, whom she herself seems to have resembled greatly, brought her up. She was taught to read, to reason, and to judge men and women fairly. Thus her education was devoted not to book learning, but to the art called *savoir vivre*, the art of living properly. " Knowledge," said her grandmother, " never made

a foolish woman wise." One could get on without
knowledge if one had only tact and address.
Grandmother herself travelled successfully through
the world on the strength of these two qualities.
She could talk most entertainingly of things of
which she knew little or nothing. When caught
in a blunder, she extricated herself so prettily that
one liked her the better for it. She cultivated the
heart, the judgment, the taste of her little granddaughter, and let mere intellect take care of itself.
The education of Madame Geoffrin was just such a
one as, knowing her, we should have supposed it
to have been.

When Madame Geoffrin, then Marie Thérèse
Rodet, was fourteen years old, she married a gentleman much older than herself and very wealthy,
Monsieur Pièrre Francois Geoffrin. He, too, was
of the bourgeois class, a lieutenant of the National
Guard, and one of the founders of glass manufacture.
He was of the chimney-corner variety of gentleman — quiet, unobtrusive, stupid. He sat silent at
madame's table full of guests. At length he was
seen no more. Some one inquired of Madame
Geoffrin, "What has become of that old gentleman
who always was present at your dinners?" "It
was my husband," she answered. "He is dead."
Outwardly, then, it would seem monsieur played
no part in madame's career. In private, however, their married life was similar to that of
many bourgeois couples, humdrum but stormless.

Madame was spared the domestic complications and disasters that so often were the portion of the women of the noble class.

It was to her husband that Madame Geoffrin was indebted for the instrument of her power. He furnished the means that were essential. Having the means, she herself established the " institution," for so her salon was called. She filled her house with beautiful pictures and statuary ; she provided her table with the choicest and most delicious of good things. This she did with refined and delicate taste, without ostentation or vulgarity. She opened her doors to savants, philosophers, artists, litterateurs, brilliant women, and laughing girls. She, a plain, plebeian woman, received these chosen spirits of her age with a manner that was at the same time respectful and pleasantly familiar. She depreciated herself, but allowed none of her guests to depreciate her. She was modest, and she was also dignified. Thus her address was perfect. With such taste, such address, and added to these infinite social talent, she was what has been fitly termed a " minister of society," a " civilizer."

Her salon was, Sainte Beuve informs us, the most complete, the best managed, the best appointed. It was, moreover, the most important. She who had neither youth, beauty, nor education to recommend her was the chief of the salonists.

We first hear of her as coming into prominence in 1748. Then she was on the eve of her fiftieth birthday. From that time on, over a period of twenty-five years, her empire continued and extended. She sat upon her throne, a regal schoolmistress, and summoned her subjects about her, and with a mingling of severity and gentleness, she told her little anecdotes and preached her little sermons and recited her clever little maxims and justly apportioned the rewards and the punishments. She was a quiet influence for good in a time when vice was very noisy.

It was not only her grandmother's teachings which had helped Madame Geoffrin to this high position. She had acquired something from Madame de Tencin. Madame Geoffrin had attended frequently the salon of that talented but immoral woman. Madame de Tencin, when she was dying, shrewdly observed, " Do you know why she comes ? It is to see what she can gather from my inventory." It was spiteful, no doubt, of Madame de Tencin to say this, and yet, as it chanced, Madame Geoffrin really did inherit, in a measure, the social sway of Madame de Tencin. She learned method from her. It was Madame de Tencin who told her, " Refuse the friendship of no man, for though nine persons out of ten should fail you the tenth may prove useful to you." This advice Madame Geoffrin remembered. Though she did not accept it wholly, she profited by it.

Madame de Tencin's method, however, and grandmamma's teachings, and Monsieur Geoffrin's

fortune were but aids. The empire was Madame
Geoffrin's by her own right, a right that came of a
wisdom not of books — something deeper, broader,
and more intuitive. This wisdom we may define
as common-sense, compounded of tact and taste
and kindness and a proper regard for order and
right conduct.

Madame's management of her salon was a fine
art. Upon it she spent infinite thought and labor—
careful thought, skilled labor. She permitted no
hitches, no jars. Consequently, all ran as smoothly
as the perfected wheelwork of an expert artisan.
On Mondays she entertained at dinner artists and
sculptors ; on Wednesdays, men of letters. At
these dinners Mademoiselle de Lespinasse was the
only woman guest. Women, Madame Geoffrin
determined, divided the interest; and what she
desired for these dinners was unity. After dinner
she received the world. Then the evening ended
with a merry little supper, to which were bidden
half a dozen or so of her most intimate friends,
this time both women and men. At her board, in
her parlors, might be seen Marmontel, Holbach,
d'Alembert. To their philosophic and literary
talk was added the broken French of some illustrious foreigner and the girlish treble of some sweet
flower of a Countess d'Egmont.

Over her guests, it has been said, Madame
Geoffrin presided like " an invisible Providence."
Her influence was one of peace. She never per-

mitted conversation to wander into the stormy
realms of politics and religion. She tolerated no
passions, not even the passion for virtue. When
discussions became in the least degree heated, she
raised her hand enjoining silence. "There, that
will do," she said, and she introduced a more
tranquil topic.

Her rule, therefore, was quiet. She would permit no rebellious pupils in her school. When one
was so naughty as to do or say or write anything
that sent him to the Bastille, she was much displeased and never quite forgave him. She did not
like extremes. "My mind," she said, "is like my
legs. I love to walk on level ground, and I do not
wish to climb a mountain to have the pleasure of
saying, when I have reached the top, 'I have
climbed that mountain.'" She was opposed to
haste and change, and though she was in favor of the
philosophic spirit of the time, she wished to keep it
within bounds. "There is no need," she declared,
" of pulling down the old house before we have built
the new one." Thus her empire was one of calm
restraint.

From all this it may be seen that Madame Geoffrin was a Conservative. She was an example of the
moderate spirit of the first half of the seventeenth
century. And she was also an example of its dry-
ness, its terseness, its practicality. She was without extravagances and without illusions. She
hated flattery, and desired always that people

should address her with the simplicity and frankness of a child. To Madame Necker she wrote: " My dear friend, I beg of you to lessen your excessive admiration. I assure you, you humiliate me. The angels think very little about me, and I do not trouble myself about them. Their praise and blame are indifferent matters to me, for I shall not come their way. But what I desire is that you love me and take me as you find me."

Madame's charity, too, was in keeping with the age which she represented, an age so moderate, so dry, so terse, so practical, that it was also egotistical. Some one once spoke disparagingly to her of her cream. " What can I do? " she said. " I cannot change my milk woman." " And why not? " inquired her friends. " What has your milk woman done that you cannot change her? " " I have given her two cows," madame replied. That was her way. Her acts of benevolence were to her works of art which she loved to contemplate. She would do nothing to spoil them and detract from the pleasure which her recollection of them afforded her. Thus her charity, while generous and kind, was not exactly according to Scripture. It sought its own. What madame desired was not so much the happiness of the recipient as her own satisfaction. She bestowed her gifts with a delicacy that made refusal a rudeness. She ran away, quite inconsiderately, from the tears and thanks of the beholden. There was a little selfishness in all this,

yet a noble selfishness that sought the realization
of goodness for its goal. Madame herself admitted
the fault in her charity, and excused it in her
usual clever fashion. Those who gave seldom, she
declared, had no need of thinking of themselves;
but those who, like herself, made a practice of
giving must do so in the way most agreeable
to themselves, for " it is necessary to do con-
veniently," she said, " what one wishes to do every
day."

Madame's charity, then, was no more angelic
than she desired Madame Necker's praises of
herself to be. It was of the earth, and very sensible and practical. We are able to trace it in a few
of its various windings. We discover Madame
Geoffrin paying the debts of Stanislaus Poniatowski, afterwards king of Poland, and granting to
Morellet a sufficient allowance for an independent
existence, and to Thomas another such allowance.
We see her visiting the houses of her friends, and
bestowing here and there a vase, a couch, a chair,
whatever is most needed. And on Sunday after-
noons, when she is alone, coming upon her by
stealth, we find her tying up little bags of money
for distribution among the poor. She had what
she called the giving humor. It was a help and
comfort to the world.

Such was Madame Geoffrin's life. She bestowed
gifts; she entertained her friends at little dinner
and supper parties; she managed her house and

her salon. Her days passed smoothly and monotonously.

At length came the event of her life. She made her journey to Warsaw. Her favorite among her school-children, Stanislaus Poniatowski, was the cause of her journey. Stanislaus, her protegé, whose debts we saw her paying, had ascended the throne of Poland. He wrote to her: "Mamma, your son is king." He invited her to visit him in his new kingdom. She accepted his invitation, she left her dear France, and this because she loved him.

Madame Geoffrin loved Stanislaus as she might have loved a son. She scolded him as she scolded all her school-children, she encouraged him, she gave him wise counsel. He endured her scoldings; he responded to her encouragements; he disregarded her counsels; he behaved as children will. She quarrelled with him and forgave him. "When one is young," she told him, "pleasures, passions, tastes even form attachments and break them. My love for you depends on none of these things, and therefore it has lasted. It has lasted in spite of candor and plain speaking, and it will last to the end of my life." She spoke truly. She loved him, as she said, to the end, and dying while he was yet prosperous was spared the pain of his downfall.

It was to visit Stanislaus, as we have seen, that Madame Geoffrin made her famous journey to

Warsaw. Her one thought was of him. She did
not anticipate the triumphs with which she was
everywhere met. The monarchs of the countries
through which she passed seemed to forget that
she was just a private citizen, and treated her
like a queen. Maria Theresa was especially atten-
tive to her. Madame Geoffrin saw at the Austrian
court Marie Antoinette, then a beautiful child of
twelve. " As lovely as an angel," Madame Geoffrin declared her to be. " Write to your country
and say you have found her so," was the answer
she received, and it was thus she wrote. Later she
wrote of the king of Poland: " It is a terrible
position to be king of Poland. I dare not say how
unfortunate I find him." She wrote, too, that her
heart remained the same. She was loyal to old
friends. Honors had not turned her head. She
found men and things much the same everywhere,
yet kept always her preference for France. " All
that I have seen since I quitted my Penates,"
she declared, "makes me thank God for having
been born a Frenchwoman and a private citizen."

Madame Geoffrin returned to Paris and the
Parisians. She was glad to be at home again,
When people spoke to her of the consideration she
had been shown, she neither denied it nor boasted
of it. She maintained her dignified and clever
modesty.

She continued her dinner and supper parties,
her scoldings, and her generous giving. She drew

from her little court the best that was in them,
whatever of virtue, whatever of talent they possessed. Once she complimented an old abbé on
his conversation. "Madame," he replied, "I am
but the instrument on which you have played
beautifully." And what the old abbé said that she
did to him she did to all. She played beautifully
on every one who came within her influence.
Consequently, there was always harmony where
she was.

Madame Geoffrin was a philosopher with the
philosophers. Yet there was a private chapel in
her mind to which her thought very often repaired.
She was quietly religious. She was disturbed
when one of her school-children died without confession, just as she was when one of them was sent
to the Bastille. She wished to have the proprieties
observed in religion as in all things. Madame
Geoffrin had a daughter, an only child, who was
more strictly, more ostentatiously devout. She
did not like her mother's philosophic friends. As
Madame Geoffrin grew old and ill and feeble,
this daughter stood sentinel over her and would
not admit Marmontel, D'Alembert, and the rest
to her mother's presence. Her severity amused
Madame Geoffrin. "My daughter is like Godfrey
de Bouillon," she said. "She wants to defend my
tomb against the infidels." She secretly continued her gifts to "these infidels," and sent them
messages of good will and affection. But she did

not see them. Thus she kept peace with her daughter, and at the same time did not forsake her friends.

We are granted a pleasant glimpse of Madame Geoffrin in these last days. She writes to Stanislaus of a visit she has just received from a troop of merry girls. She is merry with them, she laughs with them, she makes them forget the distance between youth and age. Yet, before they leave, she lets fall a bit of her school-ma'am sophistry. She scolds them for wasting their youth, and preaches to them that they may have an old age as bright and healthy as hers.

This was Madame Geoffrin. No one understood so well as she how to combine the ethical and the gay, the frowns and the smiles of life. She was a dear mentor. It is as such that the world remembers her and as such that the world loves her.

MADEMOISELLE DE LESPINASSE.

Born at Lyons, Nov. 18, 1732.
Died at Paris, May 23, 1776.

"It is impossible to encounter such beings (as Mlle. de Lespinasse), victims of a sacred passion and of so generous a woe, without being moved to a sentiment of respect and admiration in the midst of the profound pity which they inspire." — *Sainte-Beuve.*

MADEMOISELLE DE LESPINASSE, writing to that "false great man," M. de Guibert, whom she so passionately loved, compared her life to the most pathetic pages in the novels of Richardson and Prevost. "I have lived a hundred years," she said. In a sense she spoke truly. With such intensity had she existed, so much of loving and of suffering had she experienced in her short life that in spirit, if not in fact, her years numbered a hundred.

During mademoiselle's lifetime she was known only as the charming woman dear to society, the mistress of the Parisian salon most in vogue. The world that every day from five in the afternoon to nine in the evening assembled in her parlors in the Rue de Belle-Chasse was not acquainted with her other personality. It was not until after her death that her true character became manifest. Then it was that the publication of her letters by the widow

65

of Guibert, the man to whom the letters were addressed, revealed Mademoiselle de Lespinasse as she really was, a woman all feeling, all heart, a feverish, throbbing, self-consuming soul.

There was ever about Julie an atmosphere of mystery and sadness. " Her face was never young," said one who knew her. She was twenty-two years old when, as the companion of the witty, crotchety, old Madame du Deffand, she made her first appearance in Parisian society. Every one was inquiring who she was, whence she came, what was her history. That she was somebody from somewhere and that she had a history was evident to all. But no one could discover anything about her. Madame du Deffand was deaf to all questions in regard to her charming young companion. And Julie herself on all personal matters maintained a sorrowful and impenetrable silence.

People were left to wonder. They wondered. And while they wondered, they admired, they loved. This Mlle. Julie de Lespinasse, who had neither fortune, rank, nor beauty to commend her, became the rage in Parisian society. The habitués of Madame du Deffand's brilliant salon almost forgot the witty marquise whom they had come to see, and gave their thoughts and their attention to the poor, proud, untitled woman who was her companion.

All people, even those who admired and loved Julie most, found it difficult to explain her charm.

MADEMOISELLE DE LESPINASSE.
From a painting by Carmontelle.

She was not pretty they admitted. Indeed, she was quite plain, but — the "buts" came fast, eloquently, ardently.

Julie was tall and slender and of a noble, graceful bearing, we are told. The perfect taste and simplicity with which she dressed gave the effect of richness to her apparel. But her chief attraction, her chief external charm, the one upon which all testimonies agree and dwell was her "expressive countenance." She had not one expression, we are informed, but all expressions. Her voice, too, was remarkable. It had all tones, all inflections. And never, it was said, did a more perfect harmony of face, voice, and soul exist than that embodied in Mademoiselle de Lespinasse.

It was not upon external qualities, however, that mademoiselle depended principally for her charm. She pleased by her person. But she pleased much more by her mind, her character. That which one noted first of all in the mind, the character of Mademoiselle de Lespinasse was her tact, her intuitive, unerring tact. She exclaimed once to her friend, D'Alembert, "Oh, I wish that I could know everybody's pet weakness." She said this because she liked to make those about her happy, to help them to appear at their best by leading them to speak of that in which they were, each one, most interested. And, if we will examine the testimony of those who knew her, we will find that she was not far from obtaining her wish. It is related of

her that she said to each one that which suited him,
that she never talked above or below the feelings or
understandings of her listener, that she had always
at her disposal that precious gift of the right word,
that she drew confidence gently, and divined every
one's secret thoughts.

An aid to her in this power of divination was a
quality that has been defined by one among her
friends as "freedom from personality." She forgot herself, she lost herself in the interest of others.
She was no longer herself when talking. She was
somebody else's " I."

This power of divination, this ability to put herself in another's place, this exquisite tact, ranked
first among her charms. That which was next
admired, next praised, was her naturalness. She
was, we are told, natural in her bearing, her movements, her gestures, her thoughts, her expressions,
her style. Pretension was repugnant to her. And
she hated the affected manners and other follies of
people in society. She never aired her knowledge,
her talents, her abilities. Consequently it was of
her, not of these other things, that people thought
when they talked to her. It was herself they
loved.

We might go on indefinitely speaking of mademoiselle's charms, of the excellence of her tone,
the correctness of her taste, her knowledge of all
that is elegant and refined and which enabled her
to divine the language of what is called "good

society," as Pascal in his day, while it was yet unformed, divined the French language. Reading of these charms, told in the glowing phrases of her admirers, we are pleased with mademoiselle as the world of her time was pleased with her. She was so thoroughly a lady that we cannot but enjoy her company. As yet we know her only, we like her only, as the world knew and liked her. Later we shall become more intimately acquainted with her, we shall see her as her friends saw her. We shall discover what D'Alembert called "the shadows" in her character. We shall discover these shadows and at the same time, through the eyes of her friends, we shall behold lights of mind and character as yet unrevealed.

It was mademoiselle as we now know her, however, the tall, graceful, unbeautiful woman with expressive countenance, simply dressed, tactful, natural, in every point a lady, who captivated the world of the Parisian salon. For her people forsook Madame du Deffand, the wittiest and most aristocratic woman in Paris, and followed her, an emigrant spirit, to her modest little apartment in the Rue de Belle-Chasse. She was the magnet to whom poets, philosophers, students, men of fortune, and affairs were drawn.

Mademoiselle de Lespinasse certainly was a remarkable and interesting woman. It was natural that people should wonder about her, that they should wish to penetrate the atmosphere of mystery

that enveloped her. Yet few among her intimates
were admitted to her secrets. Few knew of Julie
all that there was to know.

Her history, as she herself declared, was a sad
one. She was the natural daughter of the Countess D'Albon, a lady of consequence in Burgundy.
She was brought up by her mother, loved and
cared for by her in secret, and given a brilliant
education.

It was at the time of this mother's death that
unhappiness first claimed Julie for its own. The
intimacy of family life, Guibert tells us, is the
scene of life's deepest passions and greatest calami-
ties. He said this with Julie's story in mind.
From the position of cherished daughter she
descended to that of dependent, of stranger. Her
relatives were not her friends. Rather they were
her persecutors. They told her ruthlessly who
she was and that she must expect nothing from
them. We can imagine what were the sufferings
of the proud, sensitive girl, so suddenly orphaned
and abandoned. " Sorrows," remarked D'Alembert,
referring to that period of her life, " fed upon her."

Five of the years following her mother's death
Julie lived at Chamrond with the Marquise de
Vichy, legitimate daughter of the Countess D'Albon.
She had the right to expect some privileges, some
advantages, but she was given none. Almost
immediately she was made governess of the marquise's children. Humble, inferior duties were

hers. She could have forgiven the duties, however.
The marquise's manner toward her, one of insolent
patronage, she could not forgive.

The Marquise de Vichy had married the brother
of Madame du Deffand, the Marquis de Vichy-
Chamrond. And it was at the chateau of Chamrond that Madame du Deffand and Julie de Lespinasse first met. Madame, it is said, was
impressed with the air of sadness that dimmed
the young girl's face and she was attracted by
Julie's rare charm and intelligence. The two
women were warmly drawn to each other. The
superiority of their minds made them congenial
comrades. Madame soon drew Julie's confidence.
" She told me," wrote Madame du Deffand, " that
it was no longer possible for her to remain with
Monsieur and Madame de Vichy; that she had long
borne the harshest and most humiliating treatment;
that her patience was now at an end ; that she had
declared to Madame de Vichy that she must go
away, being unable to bear any longer the scenes
that were made to her daily."

Madame du Deffand, as it happened, was at this
time nearly blind and in search of a reader, a
companion. Mademoiselle de Lespinasse, she
decided, was the person she needed, the person she
desired. She proposed to Julie that she come and
live with her in Paris at her apartment in the Con
vent of Saint Joseph. Julie could not immediately
accept the offer. Her brother and sister, the

Vicomte D'Albon and Madame de Vichy raised objections. They feared the position proposed to her might make known her rights to the D'Albon name and a share in the family fortunes. She retired to the convent at Lyons to await their consent.

Julie received many grave injunctions from Madame du Deffand in regard to the new position she was called upon to fill. Madame pictured to her what her life would be, told her it would be a dull one, reminded her that, though she would be in the world, she could not be of it, commanded that she must totally forget who she was and resolve never to think of changing her social state. Above all, madame insisted upon perfect candor in Julie's deportment toward herself. "The slightest artifice," she informed her, "even the most trifling little art, if you were to put it into your conduct, would be intolerable to me. I am naturally distrustful and all those in whom I detect slyness become suspicious to me to the point of no longer feeling the slightest confidence in them. Therefore, you must, my queen, resolve to live with me with the utmost truth and sincerity."

Julie listened. Her young, ardent, aspiring spirit grew troubled under the older woman's strictures and wisdom. Perhaps she felt that this suspicious woman of the world, who had taken so great a fancy to her mind was quite incapable of ever knowing her heart. She feared, she told madame, to fall into a state of discouragement, which would render her intolerable and inspire her future mistress with disgust and repentance. We can imagine Julie's attitude of proud humility, and the air of measured kindness and reassurance with which the elder woman met it. In the end, as was inevitable, Julie agreed, she promised. And when her brother and sister, persuaded of their own security under the conditions of her new position, had given their consent, she went to live as companion and reader to Madame du Deffand, in that worldly retreat of unworldly name, the Convent of Saint Joseph.

The life in common between Madame du Deffand and Mademoiselle de Lespinasse was begun in 1757, and it lasted ten years. Considering the natures of the two women and the elements with which they had to reckon, the amazing thing is not that their intimacy did not continue longer, but that it continued as long as it did. Given two women, such as they, of equal minds, both preeminently fitted for social leadership, the one a recognized power, old, jealous, suspicious, the other a rising sovereign, young and ambitious, a rupture was the natural, almost the inevitable, consequence of their union. It is not difficult to picture the various stages of the estrangement: madame's envy of Julie's success, the gradual withdrawal of her friendly patronage and protection, the development of her never very sweet

disposition to the point of injustice and unkind-
ness ; Julie's distress when she found herself
out of favor, her tactful, painstaking attempts
to reinstate herself in the good graces of her
mistress, then, as madame continued to play the
tyrant, the slow cooling of mademoiselle's interest
and gratitude. We are sorry for madame, and at
the same time we are sorry for Julie. Of course
both were at fault, and yet neither was at fault.
Their's was a quarrel in which it is impossible to
determine the right and the wrong.

However, when we come to consider the final
break, I think it is madame, old, sick, disappointed,
abandoned, defiant, who has our sympathy, not her
brilliant young companion whose glory has
eclipsed her own. It may be that Julie is no more
culpable than before, but she is victorious, and
sympathy always goes to the unfortunate, to the
defeated.

"The slightest artifice," madame had said to
Julie when she took the young girl to live with
her, "would be intolerable to me." In madame's
eyes Julie was found guilty of this artifice when
she entertained a chosen few of madame's friends,
privately, secretly in her own room. Madame du
Deffand, who was an invalid and who slept late,
rising unexpectedly one evening, came suddenly
upon mademoiselle and her company. Madame felt
herself robbed of her social rights, cheated, out-
raged. Her anger broke forth violently. To her

mind this secret meeting in mademoiselle's room
was nothing less than treachery. "She uttered
loud out-cries," said Marmontel, who was among
those present, "she accused the poor girl of steal-
ing her friends, and declared that she would no
longer warm the serpent in her bosom."

The rupture between the two women had all the
importance of an event. Parisian society was
divided, so to speak, into two camps. Julie's camp
had by far the greater number of followers. Not
only did D'Alembert, whom Madame du Deffand
compelled to chose between herself and her former
companion, boldly take Julie's part, not only did
those men more especially Julie's friends, such
men as Turgot, the Chevalier de Castellux, and
Marmontel stand by her, but even President Henault and others of madame's intimates declared for
Mademoiselle de Lespinasse.

Julie left the Convent of Saint Joseph abruptly.
Her separation from Madame du Deffand left her
with only the trifling income of one hundred
crowns bequeathed to her by her mother.

Though poor in purse, however, she was rich in
friends. One friend obtained for her an annual
income from the king, which placed her above
actual need. Another friend made a present to her
of the furniture of the apartment she had hired.
She found herself established, though not luxu-
riously, at least comfortably and pleasantly in the
Rue de Belle-Chasse, mistress of a salon which

culled every evening for its adornment the flower
of the minds of that time.

To advance her new position in life, many generous offers of assistance were made to Julie.
She would receive, however, only such as she
believed confidently that she could return. She
preferred being poor to being indebted. She had
what D'Alembert defined as "the honorable pride
that hates benefits."

"I have always considered," she once said to
Guibert, "that equality is the first condition to render friendship durable. Friendship cannot exist
from the moment one friend becomes the benefactor,
the other the beholden. The cares, attentions,
councils, feelings of my friends I receive because
I can return them. But how can I return what
they might do to increase my means? I should be
for the rest of my life ill at ease with them; whenever my affection worked, I should fear they saw
only my gratitude. They would love me less.
And as for me, I should feel oppressed by the sort
of ascendancy I had given them over me."

Perhaps Julie's hatred of benefits, her "honorable pride," was excessive. Yet we must agree
with D'Alembert that it was a "virtue" and
admire her for it as her friends admired her.

Mademoiselle's slender means would not permit
her to give suppers like Madame Geoffrin, Madame
Necker, and the other salonists of the day. But
every evening from four to nine o'clock she was

at home, and not for all the feasts of the Mæcenases of her time would mademoiselle's friends have missed her festivals of intellect, grace, and elegance.

Mademoiselle's salon was more intellectual than Madame du Deffand's, more aristocratic than Madame Geoffrin's. It was characterized above all else by variety. In every other salon there was some ruling spirit. In mademoiselle's not even D'Alembert was any more than an ordinary visitor. There was in mademoiselle's salon a place for every person, a chance for every topic of conversation; politics, religion, philosophy, anecdotes, and news all contributed to the entertainment of the company.

Marmontel has compared Julie's management of her salon to the wand of an enchantress. At a word, lightly thrown in, apparently without effort, she could change the talk, direct it at will, exciting it or modulating it as she desired. " Under her guidance," he said, " the variously assorted, widely differing members of society fell into harmony like the strings of an instrument touched by an able hand. She played the instrument with an art that came of genius. She seemed to know what tone each string would yield before she touched it. I mean to say that our minds and our natures were so well known to her that in order to bring them into play she had only to say a word."

Grimm wrote similarly of Julie's ability as mistress of her salon. " She possessed," he said, " in an
eminent degree that art so difficult and so precious,
— of making the best of the minds of others, of
interesting them and bringing them into play without any appearance of constraint or effort. No one
knew better how to do the honors of her house.
She had great knowledge of the world and that
species of politeness which is most agreeable ; I
mean that which has the tone of personal interest."

For her position in the world mademoiselle was
fitted, as we have seen, by nature. She had received,
moreover, in the salon of Madame du Deffand the
best sort of preparation for the part she had to
play. " See what an education I received !" she
says herself. "Madame du Deffand, President
Henault, the Abbé Bon, the Archbishop of Toulouse, the Archbishop of Aix, Monsieur Torgot,
Monsieur D'Alembert, the Abbé Boismont — these
were the persons who taught me to speak and to
think and who have deigned to consider me as
something."

Conversation was not all that went on in Julie's
salon. Academicians were made there. D'Alembert was the secretary of the institution and,
through her influence on him, mademoiselle did much
to the making of reputations and the electing of
members to the academy. Chastellux owed his
admission in a great measure to her, and on her
deathbed she secured that of La Harpe. Some

blamed mademoiselle for concerning herself in the affairs of the academy. Her friend Grimm defended her. " Why should women, who decide everything in France," he queried, "not decide the honors of literature ? "

We now know Julie as the world knew her. We have next to become acquainted with her as her most intimate friends, those who loved her best, as D'Alembert knew her, and finally as he to whom she disclosed her soul, as Monsieur de Guibert knew her.

Of all of Julie's friends, and she had many, the most appreciative among them, the most constant, the most devoted was D'Alembert—D'Alembert, the philosopher and mathematician, D'Alembert, secretary of the French Academy, chief of the Encyclopedists.   Of the connection which existed between him and Julie we may say that it was the sweetest and most beautiful episode in the lives of both. In reference to it Julie remarked, and she remarked it, sighing, for the last time, to D'Alembert a short time before she died : " Of all the feelings which I have inspired, mine for you and yours for me is the only one that has not made me unhappy."

Julie de Lespinasse and D'Alembert met for the first time in the salon of Madame du Deffand. They were immediately attracted to each other. " All things," said D'Alembert, " even our common fate, seemed destined to unite us. Both without family, without relatives, having experienced neg-

lect, misfortune, and injustice, — nature seemed to
have put us in the world to seek each other out
like two reeds which cling together and support
each other."

When Julie left Madame du Deffand and went
to live in the Rue de Belle Chasse, D'Alembert
was residing with his foster mother on the Rue
Michel-le-Comte.   The Rue Michel-le-Comte was
a long distance from the Rue de Belle Chasse, but
no matter how bad the weather, D'Alembert never
failed in his attendance at Julie's evening assem-
blies.   He was taken suddenly very ill.   Julie
went to nurse him.   If the world had been dis-
posed to criticise her for her action, which it was
not, it could not have deterred her.   In the cause
of friendship Julie was always ardent, impetuous,
careless of restriction or convention.   D'Alembert's
physician was very grave when questioned as to
his patient's condition.   He said that the air of the
Rue Michel-le-Comte, which was by no means
pure and free, might prove fatal.   Hearing this,
Julie straightway had D'Alembert removed from
the Rue Michel-le-Comte to her own lodgings.
D'Alembert recovered, but he did not change his
quarters.   He and Julie continued to live under
the same roof, in all propriety and honor, each in a
separate suite of rooms.

Malignity never attacked mademoiselle and
D'Alembert because of their intimacy.   Rather
they were the more respected, the more admired,

on account of it. There was in it something lofty
and noble. D'Alembert thus described the nature
of the union : " There is between us neither marriage nor love," he said, " only reciprocal esteem
and all the gentleness of friendship."

So far as Julie was concerned, the statement was
doubtless a fact. But of his own feelings D'Alembert was not telling the whole truth. He loved
Julie for sixteen years, loved her deeply, silently,
untiringly, and with an unselfishness very rare.

D'Alembert spoke of himself as an " old and sad
philosopher." He believed that Julie was worthy
of a younger, livelier man than he, and of a richer
establishment than he could offer her. He assumed
toward her the attitude of an elder brother. He
admired her, he criticised her, he gave her his confidence. Each morning, before setting out on some
project, some literary undertaking, he asked for her
encouragement. Each evening he returned to her
with the story of his day's doings. And Julie was
always at hand, always waiting, kind, interested,
sympathetic, an ideal sister.

Together they discussed the affairs of the
Academy, and of the Encyclopedists. They spoke
of literature. Julie talked enthusiastically of
Racine, Voltaire, and La Fontaine. She praised Le
Sage and Prevost. She grew impassioned over
Rousseau, Richardson, and Sterne, the author of the
"Sentimental Journey," which she had translated
into French. D'Alembert smiled a little at her pref-

erences. She was too much influenced, he told
her, by the presence or absence of feeling and
warmth in a work. If a book had these qualities,
he said, whatever its blemishes, however considerable these blemishes were, she could not see them ;
the book was perfect in her eyes. Feeling and
warmth, he declared, were her domain. In all that
pertained to these qualities she was never mistaken
in her judgments. She was a sentimentalist, he
said.

One would like to linger indefinitely over this
period of Julie's life, it was so calm, so peaceful,
so pleasant, so different from the storm and stress
that succeeded it. Julie and D'Alembert had been
living under the same roof as brother and sister
several years when people first began to notice a
change in Julie. She continued to entertain her
friends, the soul of every company, displaying as
before her wonderful grace and tact and charm, but
there was a nervousness, a restlessness in her manner, an occasional showing of irritability in her
temper. She grew thinner, paler, sadder than before. She became but the shadow of her former self.
Her friends grew anxious about her. Poor D'Alembert's troubled gaze followed her everywhere. He
sought to distract her from he knew not what, to
console her, to amuse her. His attempts met with
no success. He had to endure her coldness, and,
what was harder still, her fretful humors full of
gloom and bitterness.

Julie was not ignorant of the change in herself. She sought to regain the sweet, gentle nature that had been hers. When she and D'Alembert were alone together and she saw that she had pained him by some short, hasty word, she would turn to him repentant, with tears in her eyes, and humbly ask his pardon. Yet even in those rare moments of reconciliation, there was a barrier between them, a barrier which Julie's reserve had raised. Twenty times a day D'Alembert determined to approach her, to implore an explanation of the change that had come over her, but each time he was repelled by her countenance, her words, her silence.

One day he went to her with his portrait which he presented to her with the words, —

" And tell yourself sometimes when looking at me,
Of all those who love me, who loves me as he ? "

Julie received the portrait coldly, she called the words a " kindness." The term stabbed D'Alembert like a sword thrust. Why could she not see all that he was to her, all that he wished to be? He stood before her silent, wounded. Perhaps in that moment she divined something of the extent of his affection and its steadfast purpose. We can imagine the hopeless sadness of the gaze she turned upon him. " Happiness and tranquillity," she said, " are not for me except in death." It may have been that she realized the great love ther) beside her, and that she would not, could not, stretch out her hand and take it.

The secret of the change in Julie, which puzzled the world, which alarmed her friends, which D'Alembert sought in vain to understand, was not revealed until the publication of her letters to Guibert after her death. These letters are Julie's secret, they are Julie's self. In reading them we read something not found in books, we read the drama of human life as it actually happened, we read the story of a living, loving, suffering soul laid bare.

It is with this living, loving, suffering soul known only to Guibert, the undeserving man to whom the letters were addressed, that we have now to become acquainted. We hesitate on the threshold of this intimacy to which the letters admit us. It is difficult for us who live in this century, in this country, whose tastes and characters are as they are, to know how to approach Julie de Lespinasse so closely. We can criticise her, we can even smile at her in her grand passion. She is to our comprehension so monotonous, so unreal, so foreign. And yet, if we will but understand her and sympathize with her as much as possible, we will find ourselves saying with her true and faithful friend D'Alembert, " dear and unfortunate Julie," and under these two titles forgiving her faults, as he against whom she most offended forgave them.

Except as her friendship for D'Alembert may be called love, Julie was approaching middle age without having experienced the tender, or perhaps

as applied to her we should say the stormy, passion.
She had opened her salon in the Rue de Belle-Chasse
and had been entertaining there some time when
she met Monsieur de Mora, son of the Spanish ambassador at the court of France.   This Monsieur de
Mora appears to have been quite a non-pareil of all
that is most estimable and charming.   Not only
does mademoiselle, who may be supposed to have
been slightly partial, eulogize him without stint ;
all his contemporaries seem to have vied to see
who could the most eloquently praise him.

Mademoiselle de Lespinasse loved Monsieur de
Mora and Monsieur de Mora loved Mademoiselle de
Lespinasse.   Fate, however, was not kind to their
love.   Monsieur had delicate lungs.   His native
climate was ordered for him.   He left Paris August,
1772, never to return.   At the time of his departure
mademoiselle's love for him and his for her had
never been more ardent.   They had parted with
every promise of constancy and devotion.

In September of the same year mademoiselle
met the Comte de Guibert.   With the moment of
her meeting with Guibert the tragedy of her life
began — it was a struggle between her two loves,
the one for Mora, powerful, but dying slowly, re-
morsefully, the other for Guibert, impetuous, irresistible, like a torrent driving everything before it.

Monsieur de Guibert was a colonel in the French
army.   He had entered the world with his head
held high.   He was brilliant, impressive, dashing.

Society had made up its mind that he was destined for glory. Guibert himself was of society's opinion. He had published an essay on war tactics, he had competed at the Academy, he was composing trage- dies with which he intended to dazzle the world. He aimed at replacing the great writers of the past. He was a genius, he believed, and the world believed with him. Men spoke of him as "a soul which springs on all sides towards fame." He sprang, it is true, but he fell. Fame knows him now only as the man loved by Mademoiselle de Lespinasse.

The fact that Monsieur de Guibert was ten years younger than mademoiselle may perhaps shock us: But it did not shock Parisian society. In France it was the custom for young men entering the world to court the patronage of certain charming women, older and more experienced than they. The women on their part enjoyed the gallantries of the young men.

It must not be supposed from this, however, that the feelings of mademoiselle for Guibert were those of these other women for their protegés. She was not like the women of society, satisfied with being " preferred," content merely "to amuse and to please." "I live to love, I love to live," that was her motto. "I love you," she told Guibert. "All personal interest is hushed by those words. That 'I' of which Fenelon speaks is a myth. I feel in a positive manner that I am not I ; I am you, and in order to be you I have no sacrifice to make. Your interests, your happiness, your affections, your pleasure—in them, mon ami, is the I that is dear to me, that is within me ; all else is external and foreign to me. You alone in the universe can hold and occupy my being. My heart, my soul, can henceforth be filled by you alone." Such sentiments surely show that mademoiselle and her love for Guibert were far removed from the superficialities of women in society.

Julie began by believing Guibert to be all that is great and noble. It did not take her long to discover how shallow he was, how volatile, how insincere. However, the harm was done. She had given him her heart. She could not, try as she might, regain it. " The minds of most women," she exclaimed with La Rochefoucauld, "seem to strengthen their folly rather than their reason." With remorse and loathing she realized her folly, she compared the two men, de Mora, whom she had ceased to love, and Guibert, whom spite of herself she loved always and entirely. Then with clear-sighted vision she regarded Guibert. " And it is *you* who have made me guilty toward that man," she cried despairingly. "The thought revolts my soul."

At length came the death of de Mora. He died at Bordeaux. Unable to live without Julie, he was returning to her. He was faithful to the last. Julie's friends, who had divined that a very close relationship existed between her and the Spaniard, came to her with protestations of kindness and sympathy and consolation. " They do me the honor," wrote Julie, " to believe that I am crushed by the loss that I have met with." She was obliged to receive these protestations, conscious all the while that she did not deserve them. Her dissimulations with D'Alembert and others who loved her filled her with · horror. More than ever she judged her love for Guibert to be a crime. Because of it she hated herself, because of it she suffered the " tortures of the damned." And yet so dear was it to her, so much dearer than all will or reason or self-respect or happiness, that with Phyrrus she exclaimed, " I yield to the crime as a criminal."

She abandoned herself unreservedly and utterly to her passion. " This soul," she writes, " carried away by an irresistible force, finds it hard to curb and calm itself; it longs for you, it fears you, it loves you, it wanders in a wilderness, but always it belongs to you." She lived only to receive Guibert's letters and his calls, to see him and to love him. " From every instant of my life," she tells him, " I suffer, I love you, I await you." And again, " There is nothing I have not tried to cheat my impatience," she declares ; " I am perpetually in motion, I have been everywhere and seen everything and I have but one thought."

Guibert's letters were her every day desire, more necessary than her bread. " There is a certain carrier," she writes, "who for the last year gives fever to my soul." She commands that her letters be delivered to her wherever she may be. "What are you reading so earnestly?" asks an inquisitive neighbor at a dinner party. "Is it some paper for Monsieur Turgot?" "Precisely, madame," she replies. "It is a memorial I must give him presently, and I wish to read it before I give it to him."

What is in her mind as she stands there in her salon, surrounded by her friends, questioning, smiling, with an ease that has always been hers, but with an added restlessness? When the last guest has gone, and she sits alone in the late evening, writing, these are her words: "Not once has my door been opened to-day that my heart did not beat; there were moments when I dreaded to hear your name; then again I was broken-hearted at not hearing it. So many contradictions, so many conflicting emotions are true, and three words explain them: I love you." And again, "The long nights, the loss of sleep," she confesses, "have made my love a sort of madness; it has become a fixed idea, and I know not how I have escaped a score of times from uttering words that would have told the secret of my life and heart. Sometimes in society tears overtake me and I am forced to fly."

Once society had been a pleasure, a happiness to Julie. Now she no longer enjoyed it. She despised it. She spoke of it with disgust and loathing. I cannot understand the ways of people in society," she writes ; "they amuse themselves and yawn, they love no one. All that seems to me deplorable. I prefer the torture that consumes my life to the pleasure that numbs theirs." And again, " Good God," she exclaimed, "was there ever such pride, such disdain of others, such contempt, such injustice, in a word such an assemblage of all that peoples hell and lunatic asylums? All that was last night in my apartment and the walls and ceilings did not crumble down — a miracle! In the midst of the sorry writers, smatterers, fools, and pedants, I thought of you alone and of your follies ; I regretted you, I longed for you with as much passion as if you were the most amiable being in existence."

This antagonism to society is explained, as all else that is strange and incomprehensible about Julie is explained, by her love. Her love, which was her cross, her sorrow, left no room for the little joys and griefs of life. Of her successes in society she wrote, " From the moment I loved, I have felt disgust for such successes." Social disturbances no longer troubled her. She was calm and indifferent in their midst. " There is a passion of the soul," she declared, " which closes the soul to all the miseries which torture the world. A great love kills all the rest." Her past misfortune, in itself so sad, so pitiful, was forgotten. " I here avow," she declared, "that there is no sorrow comparable to that of a deep, unhappy passion. It has effaced my ten

years early torture. It seems to me that I live only
since I love. All that affected me, all that rendered
me unhappy until then is obliterated. You have
filled my life. This sorrow, it is you hath caused
it; this soul of fire and pain is your creation."

Social conventions and impossibilities were no
barriers to Julie's love. When Guibert talked of
marriage (for even in the midst of this passion he
dared to talk of marriage, alleging that he must
make a marriage of convenience, while in reality
he was planning to make one of love), she listened,
she criticised, she advised. "What I desire above
all things is your happiness," she told him, "and
the means of procuring it will be the chief interest
of my life." At length he married. Julie made
the acquaintance of his wife, praised her. The
new relationship did not abate mademoiselle's passion one whit. The immensity of her love would
admit of no boundary, no limit.

Julie's love had robbed her of her will, her reason,
her self-respect, her happiness. Gradually it was
destroying her life. "The ills of my soul have
passed to my body," she writes; "I have fever daily,
and my physician, who is the most skilful of men,
departs, saying: "We have no remedies for the
soul."

Her friends, seeing the "eternal separation," as
she expressed it, so near, gathered round her.
Looking into their faces, receiving from them their
final attentions and devotions, Julie felt that she

was beholding clear sky, that she was nearing port. Yet her passion held her still. To Guibert on her last day she said : " If ever I should return to life, I would again employ it in loving you."

On the night of her death, we are told, all her intimate friends were assembled in her room, and " all were weeping." One wonders whether Guibert was not the loudest in his grief. We know that D'Alembert was the quietest. D'Alembert as he knelt by her bed, dejected, dismayed, and bent his ear to catch her whispered word, her petition for pardon, was thinking : " She no longer has the strength to speak or to hear me. I am forced like Phedre to deprive myself of tears that might trouble her last moments. I am losing without recovery the moment of my life which might be to me the most precious, that of telling her once more how dear she is to me, how much I share her woes, and how deeply I desire to end my life with hers. I would give all the moments that remain to me to be able in this instant to show her all the tenderness of my heart in the hope of regaining hers."

Guibert lamented Julie's death with extravagant eulogy. He mourned her as deeply as one of his shallow nature could mourn.

D'Alembert was unconsoled and unconsolable in his loss. With Julie gone from his life, he felt, as he himself expressed it, " alone in the universe." Each time that he returned to his sad dwelling his thought was, "No one is waiting for me, no one will ever wait for me again."

Thus ends the story of Julie de Lespinasse, a twofold romance, sweet, tender, sorrowful. And she, the heroine, fades from before our eyes, yet seems to leave behind a light bright and pervasive like the aureole. We recognize it as the light of genius; for it has been truly said that such love as constituted the life of Mademoiselle de Lespinasse is a form of genius.

MADAME ROLAND.

Born at Paris, March 18, 1754.
Died at Paris on the guillotine, Nov. 8, 1792.

" Madame Roland is still the heroine of the Revolution. It is to her that the eye instinctively turns for a type and symbol of the earlier and finer characteristics of that movement. She was the genius and inspirer of the men whose eloquence over-threw the throne and founded the Republic." — *Edward Gilpin Johnson.*

I.

THE GIRLHOOD OF MADAME ROLAND.

MANON PHLIPON shrugged her shoulders, pouted, and averted her eyes from her parents, sitting in judgment upon her, to the world of Paris as it surged back and forth, lounging, trading, pleasure-seeking on the Pont Neuf beneath her window. It was the eternal question that was being urged — her marriage. This time papa would have her accept the proposals of some trades-man. Her foot tapped the floor indignantly. Her eyebrows went up contemptuously. Had she read Plutarch and the philosophers only to become the wife of a man bent upon getting rich and on cut-ting a good figure in his quarter?

94

MADAME ROLAND.
From a painting by Goupil.

At length papa's voice sounded behind her, puzzled, ironic, and withal amused. " What kind of a man *will* suit you, Manon ? " he inquired.

Manon turned from the window and faced her father. She was an intrepid looking little woman, short in stature, but of an erect, dauntless carriage. Of delicate, spirited features, dark-eyed, dark-haired, with a fresh color glowing in her cheeks, and of a pretty roundness of figure, she was as handsome as she was intrepid looking.

" I don't know, papa," she answered, " but it will never be any one with whom I cannot share my thoughts and sentiments. I believe there is no happiness in marriage except where hearts are closely united." As she spoke directly, earnestly, enthusiasm and a multitude of youthful dreams and fancies were shining in her eyes.

Monsieur Phlipon, however, did not see the enthusiasm, the youthful dreams and fancies. And had he seen them, he would not have understood; his soul inhabited another region than that in which his daughter's had its dwelling. He ran his fingers perplexedly through his hair.

" You think there is no one in business good enough for you," he demurred. " Is it a lawyer that you want? Women are never happy with such men; they are bad tempered and have very little money."

" But, papa," interposed his daughter, with a slight gesture of impatience, " I shall never marry anybody for his gown. I don't mean to say that I want a man of such and such a profession, but a man that I can love."

" If I understand you, you believe that such a man cannot be found in business."

" I confess that seems to me very probable. I have never found any one there to my taste. And then, business itself disgusts me."

The furrows deepened on Monsieur Phlipon's brow. " Nevertheless," he asserted, " it is a very pleasant thing to live tranquilly at home, while one's husband carries on a good business. Look at L.'s wife. Don't you think that she is happy? Her husband has just gone out of business. He has bought a large property. Their house is well kept. They see a great deal of good society."

" I cannot judge of the happiness of others," Manon sighed, wearily. " Mine, however, will never depend on wealth."

Her father rose from his chair. It appeared he had had enough of this foolish talk.

" You are making matters very difficult for your-self, Manon," he said, a little sternly. " What if you do not find your ideal? "

" I shall die an old maid," was the unflinching reply.

" Perhaps that will be harder than you think. However, you still have time. But remember, one day you will be alone, the crowd of suitors will end — you know the fable."

"Oh, I shall revenge myself by meriting happiness; injustice cannot deprive me of it."

Monsieur Phlipon lifted his eyes. "Oh, there you go in the clouds," he exclaimed despairingly, compassionately. Abruptly he left the room.

Alone with her mother, Manon drew a hassock to her mother's feet, seated herself upon it, and gazed up lovingly, a bit contritely into Madame Phlipon's face.

"Do you, too, think me a naughty, stubborn girl?" she queried. "Do you, too, believe that it is my duty to marry this man whom I do not love?"

Madame Phlipon did not answer immediately. She sat looking with a melancholy tenderness into the earnest face upturned to hers. With a gentle caress, rare in a woman of her undemonstrative nature, she touched her daughter's cheek.

"He has a great reputation for integrity and regular habits," she urged. "He is acquainted with your singular ways of thinking, professes high esteem for you, and will be proud to follow your counsels." And in a lighter, almost a playful tone, she added, "You will have him in leading strings, my dear."

Manon pouted and dropped her eyes, fingering the border of her mother's apron. "But I do not want a husband that must be led," she protested. "He would be too unwieldly a child."

Her mother smiled. "You are a funny girl, Manon," she said. "You will not have a master, yet you will not rule."

" Understand me, dear mamma," quickly, eagerly,
interposed the girl. " I would marry a man worthy of my esteem, one with whose will a compliance would be no disgrace to me and who would
not find his happiness lessened by complying with
mine."

Madame Phlipon sighed and shook her head
doubtfully. " Not so often as you imagine, my
dear child, is happiness composed of this perfection
of congeniality. If happiness depended upon nothing else, there would be little of it found in our
marriages."

" Then there would be few that I should envy,"
declared Manon in her most decisive tone.

" Perhaps not," acquiesced her mother. " And
yet, among the marriages that you despise, there
may be many preferable to a single state." Madame Phlipon's gaze wandered from her daughter.
A strange, far-away look was in her eyes. And
when she spoke again, which was after a brief
pause, it was in a sad voice, but very quietly and
gently. " I may be called out of the world soon,"
she said. " You will be left alone with your father.
He is still young. Many changes may occur in
the home where you have been so happy. My tenderness makes me fear for you. It would make my
last moments easy could I see you married before I
die to a worthy man."

Madame Phlipon's words terrified Manon. She
had not thought of the future, or of the possibility

of losing her mother; her mother who was dearer to her than her own life. She sat motionless, gazing at her mother in an agony of new-born doubts and fears.

Her mother, seeing the trouble in her eyes, sought to comfort her, and turned upon her a faint, reassuring smile. Before the smile, Manon's self-control gave way. She knelt beside her mother and clung to her, weeping passionately.

"Why are you so alarmed, my dear child?" asked her mother calmly, soothingly. "We must weigh possibilities. In health we must provide ourselves with consolations for the time of sickness and death. The present occasion furnishes us with an opportunity for such consolation. A worthy man offers you his hand. You will not always have me with you. Do not reject a husband who, it is true, may not be your ideal, but who will love and cherish you, and with whom you may be happy."

Manon lifted her head from her mother's shoulder and gazed at her sorrowfully through her tears. "Yes, my dear mamma," she exclaimed in gentle irony, "as happy as you have been!"

Madame Phlipon could make no reply. Manon had arrived at the unanswerable. Madame must hold her peace. She pressed her hands tremulously together and looked away. She had expressed herself for the last time upon the subject of Manon's marriage. Never did she refer to it again.

Manon had spoken impetuously, like one impelled by a sudden and strong conviction. She
had always been a silent witness of the disparity
that existed between her parents. But the perfect
peace that reigned in her home had seemed to her
the symbol of happiness. It was not until recently,
when her own dawning womanhood was quicken-
ing her powers of perception and understanding,
that she had come to realize at what a cost her
mother was maintaining this domestic calm. She
observed that, in the family discussions, when her
mother was unable to carry her point, she appeared
to yield it, without a scruple — and this, when she
was unquestionably in the right. Manon's love of
justice was violated, her indignation was aroused.
She constituted herself her mother's " watch-dog,"
as she expressed it. She took her part in the family debates, became her sturdy and unflinching
advocate. Yet it was only when the family was
united that Manon assumed the partisan rôle. In
his absence Monsieur Phlipon was nothing less
than the beloved husband and father. Manon and
her mother never spoke of him except in commen-
dation. "Yes, my dear mamma, as happy as you
have been!" Those words, that tone of irony,
were Manon's first criticism of her father. And by
her silence, her tremulous gesture, and her averted
glance, for the first time Madame Phlipon reproached her husband.

It must not be supposed, however, because of

this cloud that overhung the Phlipon home, that the sun did not shine there. The Phlipons had their sunshine as well as other folks. One has only to read that charming record of a girlhood, which Manon wrote in later days behind her prison bars, to appreciate the pleasant, cheerful, serene beauty of that sunshine. It is a delight to pass into its beauty with Manon, to make the acquaintance of her family and friends, to become the confidant of her high thoughts and her romantic visions, to live with her her active, intelligent, and truly noble life.

Manon spoke of herself as a child of the Seine. The house in which her father, an engraver by trade, had his shop and dwelling faced the river and looked upon the ever new and ever shifting pictures of the Pont Neuf and the Quai de l'Horloge. Her own little window opened to the north. Before it, at the close of every day, Manon kneeled. Her eyes sought the vast expanse of blue, stretching from the cool east to the west, where the roofs and tree-tops of Chaillot were glowing in the warmth of the setting sun. The view of the heavens, the sense of God's nearness, and joy in her own existence awoke in her young soul an emotion so overwhelming that tears filled her eyes. She felt the gift of her life to be inexpressibly precious. She longed to make of it something strong and noble. Her imagination soared to the heights where the martyrs and heroes had trod.

We may be grateful for this glimpse of Manon kneeling at her chamber window. We are beholding a great spirit in its early spring, its "time of blossoming," its "hour of beauty," as the Greeks called it. Manon came, in time, to climb those heights whither her imagination was so loftily pointing her the way. We shall admire her when she has attained those heights. Yet will we ever find her so lovable, so pure, so utterly unworldly and unspoiled as now?

Marie Jeanne Phlipon, as she was christened, was a heroic little person. But, we are glad to discover, she was as real and natural as she was heroic. She had her times of being naughty like ordinary little girls. At such times it was not her father's whippings that reformed her. It was the word "mademoiselle" spoken by her mother in a stern tone and with a displeased expression. The whippings Manon received in silent indignation. But to hear herself called "mademoiselle" in that tone, with that accompanying look, she could not endure. In order to bring back the smile to her mother's face and the tenderness to her voice, and to hear again the fond little nickname "Manon," she became at once a repentant and obedient daughter.

By the time she was four years old Manon had learned to read. Her parents were delighted with her precocity. She was their only child, their chief interest. They spared no pains to give her an excellent education. She was placed under the instruction of able masters, one to teach her writing, history, and geography, another for the piano, another for the guitar, another for dancing. Her father himself taught her drawing.

Manon found learning a pleasure. Often in the early morning, impelled by her thirst for knowledge, she would steal out of bed and into the alcove that opened out of the family parlor and that served as her study. There she would sit, barefooted, clothed only in her little night-gown, conning her lessons and writing her exercises.

Madame Phlipon was a devout Catholic, and Manon early received her instruction in church ritual. She was sent to the catechism class at the parish church, and, to the delight of her uncle Bimont, a young curé of the parish, in charge of the class, she carried off all the prizes. Several amusing stories are told apropos of her "theological erudition." In one of these stories we behold Manon calmly and glibly recounting the order of spirits in the celestial hierarchy. We are not surprised to hear that the eyes of the visiting rector opened wide in amazement. In another story Manon appears, a charming brunette little maiden, perched on the knee of her father's guest, relating with a solemnity suitable to the subject, the whole of the Athanasian creed. Truly the child merited her reward, which came in the form of a narration by her father's guest, of the wonderful

tale of Tanger whose nose was so long that he was
obliged, when he walked, to twist it round his
arm. It is a relief to find Manon making the
acquaintance of this gentleman of fabulous nose.
He must have been something of a comfort after
the creeds and spirits and celestial hierarchy with
which her infant mind was fed.

At the same time that Manon was learning all
that her masters and the young curé, her uncle
could teach her, she was receiving instruction of
another sort from her mother. She was being
initiated in the arts and crafts of the kitchen.
She made omelets, she picked herbs, she skimmed
the pot, and many a morning saw her trudging to
the greengrocer's and purchasing, in that sedate
manner which she had borrowed from her mamma,
the parsley or the salad that the servant had forgotten.

When Manon went to the greengrocer's she was
always very plainly dressed. But on Sundays and
fête days she appeared in the costume of a truly
"grand" lady. Little girls in her day and in her
quarter did not dress like little girls; they were
their mammas in miniature. Tight-fitting waist,
long train, and fancy trimmings were the essentials
of Manon's "Sunday best." On Sundays Manon
carried her prayer-book in her hand, and on those
fête days that meant a birthday or a wedding, or
a christening in the family, she took with her
some sample of her own work, a head that she had

drawn, or a copperplate engraving accompanied with complimentary verse and nosegay.

Outwardly, you see, Manon's life was very simple and humdrum, similar to that of any member of her class, a class which at that time was called the "bourgeois" of Paris. It was only inwardly, in that which had to do with her thoughts, her mind, her spirit, that her life was at all remarkable.

Manon's chief stimulus to this inner life that she was leading came from her reading. She loved her books. Nothing but the promise of a flower could tempt her from them. Her father's library offered attractions of a most conglomerate sort — a history of Turkey, a treatise on heraldry, the "Memoirs of Mademoiselle de Montpensier," the "Civil Wars of Appias," the Bible in old French, of which she was very fond, and the "Lives of the Saints." This latter volume was a great favorite with her. She used to dream over its pages, sighing for the times when the Christians, oppressed and persecuted by the pagans, attained the glory of the martyr's crown.

Her father's library, however, could not satisfy Manon. Having conquered the little world of literature therein contained, like Alexander, she looked about for other and greater worlds. One among her father's apprentices, it chanced, was a reader. He used to bring his books to the shop with him and keep them in a secret corner of the studio, the "atelier" the room was called. In a happy moment Manon discovered the secret

corner. Then began a course of stealthy and
systematic borrowing. One by one Manon took
the books and read them and returned them. If
the young man was aware that his secret corner
had a constant visitor, he kept the knowledge to
himself. Manon was permitted to go on her way,
along the path of knowledge, unmolested. Thus
she became acquainted with Fenélon and Tasso
and portions of Voltaire, and with a book that
took possession of her soul as no other book had
ever done. This book was " Plutarch's Lives."
As she read she became the disciple of Cato and
Socrates and Brutus. She was a republican
with them. The book was her constant companion. On Sundays, even, she could not be parted
from it, and all through one Lent she carried
it to church with her, in lieu of her prayer-book,
and read it during service.

Close intercourse with the Christian saints and
the heroes of antiquity, with lives spent in self-
abnegation and in the pursuit of high ideals, produced in Manon a state of exaltation and spiritual
awe. The mystical rites of the church appealed
deeply to her. As the time for her first communion
drew near, and its solemn meaning was impressed
upon her by friends and curé, she aspired to prepare herself by some act of devotion and sacrifice.
Separation from her mother seemed to her the
heaviest cross and so, she came to the conclusion,
that was the one that she must take up and carry.

One evening she surprised her parents by appearing suddenly before them and tearfully, zealously imploring that she be permitted to enter a convent and prepare for the sacrament.

Thus it happened that Manon Phlipon became an inmate of the Congregation. For a year she dwelt in its pure, serene atmosphere, continuing with her studies, winning the love of the young girls, her schoolmates, and of the holy sisters, her directors, and coming in time, after a period of prayer and meditation and exhortation, to receive her first communion. Her hours of recreation she used to pass reading and dreaming in the quiet convent garden, amid the breezes and the bright foliage and the sweet-smelling flowers. Often she would leave the garden to kneel in the dimly lighted chapel and listen to the chanting of the choir and the roll of the organ, and at such times, her heart full of gratitude and adoration, would speak a silent word to God.

Manon was of too serious a nature to make friends readily. For the first part of her stay at the Congregation her only intimate was Sister Agathe, one of the lay sisters, who served Manon at table, and made her bed, and was kindness itself to her. She admitted Manon to the privacy of her little cell, to her books and her canary. There was something very pretty in this friendship between Manon and the poor nun. It is pleasant to know that it endured to the close of Manon's life and was a comfort to her in the dark days just before the end.

The chief friendship of Manon's convent days, however, was not this one with Sister Agathe. It was with a young girl who came to the Congregation when Manon had been living there some months. The girl's name was Sophie Cannet. She arrived at the convent one evening with her sister. Manon was first attracted to her because of the sensibility she showed in parting from her mother. Later, as she came to know Sophie better, she loved her for her calmness and her coolness and her intelligence of mind. She did not like Henriette, the other sister, so well; she was older and she was gay and frivolous, almost too much so, Manon thought. Manon attached herself to Sophie with all the fervor of her fervent nature. In the society of others she had always worn a "veil," as she expressed it. With Sophie she put off the veil; she was frankness itself. Sophie was devout like Manon and as serious-minded as she. In character and tastes the two girls were very congenial. They worked and read and talked together. Their attachment was an ideal one, in which whatever was most intimate, most intellectual, most spiritual in the lives of both was shared. They lived, one might say, each in the other's thoughts. Throughout the convent they came to be known as "the inseparables."

At length Manon's year of residence at the Con-

gregation drew to a close. Manon did not leave
the convent without regrets, regrets for those
whom she was leaving, the sisterhood of nuns, the
devoted Agathe, and her beloved Sophie. There
were tears when the final parting came, promises
of reunion, and protestations of enduring affection.

Manon returned to her parents and to the world.
She carried away from the convent with her a
strengthened faith and piety, and a secret resolve
that, when she came of age, she would consecrate
herself to the religious life. Saint Francis of Sales
had made a conquest of her heart. She determined to make him her patron.

Circumstances, however, were conspiring to turn
Manon from her choice of the religious life. The
world was before her. Distractions, pleasures, and
a wider range of reading were awaiting her. She
was entering her teens, she was opening her eyes,
she was touching life at various points and discovering its complex character.

On Sundays and fête days Manon went to walk
with her papa in the Bois de Boulogne and the
alleys of Saint Cloud. She could not but observe
that the people whom she met regarded her with
admiration. She heard their flattering comments.
She awoke to the fact that she was pretty.

Monsieur Phlipon, as may be imagined, was
very proud of his attractive young companion. He
always introduced her with a flourish. " This is
my daughter," he would proclaim with an air of

triumph, and when she spoke, his expression seemed to say, " There! Is n't she bright? Is n't she clever?" His pride touched yet embarrassed Manon. She was glad of it, as a proof of his love for her, but she wished that it was not so evident.

Manon could forgive her father's pride in her, but she could not forgive the vanity which she discovered taking root in her own heart. After these pleasure-walks with her papa, she sat in judgment on herself. With a contemptuous shrug, she admitted that she had been elated by the admiring glances, the flattering comments of the crowd, that she had been happy in the consciousness of her becoming holiday attire and ner own good looks. Stern little moralist, she scorned herself. Had she been born, endowed with mind and soul, merely to glitter to the eye like the flowers of a parterre? In righteous wrath she determined to make war upon this " enemy " of hers, this vanity. She swore against it "implacable hostility." She " traced it in its windings." She entered upon a holy crusade against " the abominable me."

When on the next fête day papa proposed a jaunt to St. Cloud, she shook her head.

" The fountains are to play. There will be a world of company," he urged.

But the little stoic shook her head. " Dear papa," she said, " I would like better to go to Mendon."

At Mendon nature ran wild. There a forest of trees was to be found, the branches of the spotted fern, and the flowers of the gay woodbine. The place had few visitors save the birds and the swift-footed fawns. Manon loved Mendon, its solitude and its uncultivated beauty. While her father and mother lay taking their naps on the turf and the fallen leaves, she sat beside them watching the lights and shadows, learning the lessons taught by the trees and the flowers. At such moments she was nearer in spirit to the mysticism of the convent than to the glitter of St. Cloud. She had slain her "implacable" enemy—vanity. She was triumphant over the "abominable me."

Spite of these soul-inspiring sojourns to Mendon, however, and spite of her triumphant stoicism, the world continued to close about Manon. Her visits with her relatives, as well as her walks to St. Cloud, were showing her life. She was learning to know people, their relations to one another, their various ranks and grades.

Much of Manon's time was spent with her grandma Phlipon, on the island of St. Louis. The grandma was a bright, gay, vivacious little lady. Manon was very fond of her. One day grandma and granddaughter went together to make a call upon a rich and so-called "great" lady, in whose house the grandma had once been a governess. Manon observed that the servants of the house dared to compliment her in what seemed to her a too familiar manner; that the great lady seated under her "canopy," berouged, beruffled, and be-

wigged, " presumed," so Manon termed it, to pat-
ronize her and her grandmamma.   Her republican
little soul was stirred.   She averted her eyes from
the servants and the great lady, and studied the
furniture and the decorations of the room.

"You have a lucky hand," said the great lady,
Madame de Boismorel, to Manon.   " Did you ever
try it in a lottery?"

"Never, madame, I am not fond of gaming."

"So!   Indeed!   'T is a serious little girl this.
You are of a devotional turn, are you not, my
dear?"

"I know my duty to God, and I try to do it."

"That is a good girl.   You wish to take the veil,
is it not so?"

"I do not know my secret destiny and I do not
seek to penetrate it."

Manon's cheeks were flaming, her heart was
thumping violently.   What right had this vain,
vulgar person to pry into her innermost life, to
treat her noble sentiments so coldly and ironically?   She was relieved, indeed, when at length
grandma rose from her chair, and she knew that
the call was at an end.

On the way home she did not once refer to the
call, but she thought a great deal about it.   Then
there was in the world a superiority other than that
of virtue and talent, she reflected.   She and her
grandma, it appeared, were the inferiors of that disagreeable woman; they had been subjected to her

patronage, a patronage which her grandma seemed not to mind, but to accept rather as her just due. Manon knew not what to make of it all. She was indignant, she was rebellious. Alone in her own room she hurried to her books and sought to forget in reading of " the good and the true " what she had seen demonstrated of " the wrong and the untrue."

But she could not be forever reading, forever sitting grave and thoughtful in her little room. She must live with the rest of the world, and living, she must behold the vanities that were on every side. She went with her mother and her uncle Bimont to the court at Versailles. Through the courtesy of her masters and her relatives she attended the gatherings of *belle esprits* so prevalent at Paris. Everywhere she saw things to shock and disgust her. She criticised the grandeur of the king, the extravagance of court institutions, and decided that " had she been given a choice before coming into the world, she would have chosen a republic in preference to a kingdom." She turned up her nose at much that came under her notice in the gatherings of *belle esprits*. She immediately detected the pretention and conceit of those who read verses and portraits, and the insincerity of those who applauded. Yet little by little, her lofty contempt was abating. As she grew in worldly wisdom, she grew more tolerant. " The longer I live the more I study and observe," she declared ; " the more

deeply I feel that we ought to be indulgent to our
fellows."

The truth was, Manon had become a very
rational and free-thinking young woman. She
had departed a long distance from the mysticism of
her convent days. She had passed through all
stages of religious belief, had been in turn Jansen-
ist, deist, theist, sceptic, and idealist. At length
she had attained a broad, philosophic state of mind
which she never forsook. She believed in God
and the immortality of the soul. These were her
only dogmas and they made her happy. She was
convinced that it was to her own and her neighbor's interest to do right. This was her only moral
code and it made her virtuous.

It was by reading that Manon was helped to
that broad philosophic state of mind which she
had attained. Manon was everywhere on the look-
out for books, at the houses of her friends, at the
circulating libraries. She read widely, she read
intelligently. Her curé, anxious to preserve the
faith of his young parishioner, lent her the works
of the defenders of the church. She read them
and then, when she had finished, she turned her
attention to the books which these defenders of the
church refuted, the productions of Diderot,
d'Alembert and Raynal, the literature of the
encyclopedists. Dogmatic and philosophic thought
interested her especially. But she enjoyed also
that which was distinctly literary. She read

Bossuet, Fenélon, Madame de Sevigné, and Don Quixote.

Some of Manon's pleasantest reading was done during numerous backgammon parties at the house of a certain abbé, a friend of her uncle Bimont. While her mother and uncle were engaged agreeably at the board with the abbé and his housekeeper, Manon browsed in the abbé's library. She found many rare treats among his books. Therefore, though she disliked card playing, she was always sorry when the game of backgammon came to an end and the time to go home arrived.

Reading, it should be noted, was not a pastime with Manon. It was a serious business, a self-educating process to which her vigorous mind lent itself naturally. She took notes of what she read, meditated thereon, and discussed salient points with her friends. In this way she "converted into her own substance," as she herself expressed it, the thoughts of the great writers; she "became permeated with their essence."

Manon's letters to Sophie were filled with extracts from her reading and the reflections her reading awakened. Manon's letters to Sophie! Yes, for Manon and Sophie no longer talked with each other except by letter. Sophie had left the convent and Paris. She had returned to her home at Amiens. Before she went, however, the mothers of the two girls had met and "consecrated," so to speak, with their approval the friendship of their daughters. With the apparent frivolousness of maturity the mothers had smiled when the girls were solemnly vowing never to forget each other, but to love each other always with the same warmth and devotion. Of course Manon and Sophie, from what seemed to them their superior heights of wisdom, had regarded their mothers indignantly and renewed their vows with even greater fervor.

Manon and Sophie were separated. Letters were their only medium, their one means of conversation. The letters fairly flew between them. They throbbed and thrilled with a tumult of girlish thoughts, feelings, and ideals. Manon's very life was put on paper and dispatched to her dearest Sophie, her life and her ever present, ever absorbing love. She watched for the postman with the impatience of a lover and, when the letter from Amiens arrived, she could never delay its reading, but must open and devour it wherever she happened to be when it was delivered. Occasionally this was at the dinner table. She forgot where she was and shed tears over the sentimental passages. Papa and mamma smiled. From the opposite side of the table came these words in Grandma Phlipon's terse tones: "When you have a husband and children, my dear Manon, this friendship will soon vanish and you will think no more of Mademoiselle Cannet."

Manon, afterwards describing the scene to

Sophie, expressed her revolt at grandma's impossible idea.

" It surprises me," she declared, " to find that so many people regard friendship as a frivolous and chimerical sentiment. Almost every one seems to imagine that the lightest emotion of another sort is capable of changing and effacing it. They consider it the mere makeshift of an unoccupied heart. Do you believe, Sophie," she inquired fondly, rhetorically, " that any change of circumstances would break the tie between us ? "

It is a pleasure to know Manon as she appears in these letters to Sophie; she is so warm and human. One forgets for the moment the pedestaled position to which she later ascended. Sometimes, it is true, her great aspiring nature asserts itself and she impulsively exclaims, " Come to Paris, Sophie; there is nothing like residence in a place where art and science, the presence of great men, and all sorts of intellectual resources, concur and vie with one another. How interesting it would be for us to study and walk together. How I desire to know men of ability of every sort. Sometimes I feel tempted to don a hat and breeches, for the sake of being free to look about and discover what is best in all orders of talent. I have heard tales of women assuming such a disguise from motives of affection or self-sacrifice. Ah, if I were a little less rational and circumstances were a little more in my favor I swear that I have the requisite zeal."

For the most part, however, she lived very contentedly in the twilight atmosphere of her home, the "back shop," the "entresol," as she playfully designated her humble surroundings. She walks with her papa. She reads and sews with her mamma. She studies in her little closet. She thinks of Sophie, her absent friend, and sings her praises to the accompaniment of her guitar.

Now and then an interesting anecdote varies the peaceful but monotonous story of her life. She visits the painter Greuze in his studio and is charmed with his picture "The Broken Pitcher." She can find but one fault with the painting — he has not made his little one sorrowful enough to prevent her going back to the fountain. She tells Greuze this and her pleasantry amuses him. She tries to see Rousseau. Overflowing with girlish enthusiasm she welcomes the first opportunity that promises a glimpse of him, her "chiefest" hero. A friend of her father wishes to propose to the illustrious philosopher the composition of a few musical airs. Eagerly Manon undertakes the commission, writes a charming letter to her hero, and naïvely announces that she will call for the answer. Behold her, then, climbing the long, narrow stairway of the house in the Rue Plâtrière and tremblingly, reverently knocking on the door. She feels that she is standing at the entrance of a temple. The severe Thérèse clad in round cap, simple house gown, and big apron opens to her. "No" is the answer to every question which the fervent little worshipper inquires. Manon is forced to retire without so much as a glimpse of her adored philosopher.

It is a life such as this, healthful, natural, happy, that the letters to Sophie reflect. At length there steals into them a new strain, sighing, plaintive, and insistent, the theme of Manon's lovers. Manon's early piety has become an incident of the past. Her native vanity, against which she had once so vigorously struggled, and her love of attention are supreme. "From the moment," she says in her Memoirs, "when a girl attains her development, a swarm of suitors attends her footsteps, like the bees that buzz about an opening flower."

Half mockingly, half vauntingly she causes her lovers to defile before us. They come, a motley throng, very like the characters in some comic opera, of all grades and trades, the music master, the dealer in diamonds, the rising young doctor, and even the family butcher, apparently all the eligible bachelors and widowers of the Place Dauphine. Indeed, so numerous are they that we are inclined to surmise that some are there merely by reason of the heroine's creative fancy.

Such are her lovers as they appear in her Memoirs. In her letters they do not come so in a mass, but individually, and therefore they appear to be more real. Manon is satirical on the subject of her suitors, she makes herself merry over them and laughter at their expense rings through her letters.

Nevertheless they vex her. The feelings they awaken in her puzzle her. " My sentiments strike me as very odd," she says. " What can be stranger than for me to hate any one because he loves me, and from the moment I try to love him? Yet so it is." The truth is, Manon is very happy in her home, with her books and in the companionship of her mother. She has no wish to marry.

The time, however, is approaching when Manon will not be so happy. Sorrows are in store for her as for every woman who has ceased to be a girl. Her devoted mother, as we have seen, sought to prepare her for these sorrows and urged matrimony upon her as a shield against them. Until that moment when her mother spoke, Manon, secure in present joy, without a thought of future pain or separation, had wept at her mother's warning. Never again did she or Madame Phlipon renew the conversation that had been a sad one for them both. Apparently their lives were as peaceful and happy as before. Yet there was a difference, an added tenderness on the mother's part, a newly awakened anxiety on the daughter's; the thought of the future was in the mind of each. Manon especially was changed. She was constantly beset with apprehensions for her mother's health. She followed Madame Phlipon about with a newly awakened sense of responsibility. Her childlike carelessness of spirit had departed, not to return.

Indeed, so concerned was Manon that her anxiety was present even in her dreams. One night, the eve of Whitsuntide, her dreams were especially troubled. In them, it seemed to her, some danger was threatening her mother. She was wakened by a hand gently laid on her arm and a voice, her mother's, softly speaking her name. She stretched out her arms glad to be awake and to have her mother safe at her side. The day, being a fête day, Whitsuntide, was spent at Mendon. Manon and her father and mother once more enjoyed together the forest shade, the woodbine, and the spotted fern and all the beauties of their favorite retreat.

They returned to the city on Tuesday. On the next day, Wednesday, Manon and her mother had planned to make a call. When the time came, however, Madame Phlipon was too tired to go. She sent Manon without her in the care of the servant. Manon set out feeling anxious on her mother's account. She made her call very brief. All the while she was thinking of her mother, dreading that she might be ill, longing to see her and assure herself that she was well. She hurried home regardless of the servant's connotative remark that the weather was extremely favorable for a walk in the gardens.

At the doorway of her house she was met with the news which she had been fearing: her mamma had been taken ill. Manon hastened up the stair-

way to her mother's room. The attendants who
were at Madame Phlipon's side made way for the
pale girl as she entered. The sick woman's
face lighted a moment in recognition. But she
could not speak, she could not move; paralysis
had deprived her of all power of action.

Manon was immediately beside her mother, caring for her, giving orders and carrying out these
orders before another could execute them for her.
She held the candles while the priest administered
the extreme unction. She stood at the foot of the
bed and kept her eyes fixed steadfastly on the face
of her adored and dying mother. It was all a
dream, she told herself, one of those hideous
nightmares, from which she would wake to feel
again the gentle touch of her mother's hand, to
hear again the soft tones of her mother's voice
speaking her name, " Manon."

After the end they took Manon away, and tried
to make her understand that her mother was dead.
But Manon would not believe them. It was too
terrible. She could not believe them. At length
the blessing of unconsciousness came to her. She
forgot all in a dreamless sleep.

She woke at last, understanding. She had been
very ill. She was still weak. Every one was kind
to her. They came to see her, bringing books and
flowers — her father among the rest. Monsieur
Phlipon talked to her with good enough intentions,
but in a way that made her feel his distance from

her. She told herself sadly that she was completely an orphan. Her life was very empty, she reflected, she was quite alone.

It was during the dark days following her mother's death and her own illness that Manon first came to know the work of Rousseau intimately. She previously had had some acquaintance with him. She had read him, but she had read him critically. Now life was changed for her. She herself was changed. Rousseau was the food which her soul craved. She turned to him as in her early childhood she had turned to Plutarch. She found that he expressed what she herself had vaguely felt, he voiced her thoughts and sentiments. Her reading of the "Nouvelle Heloise" took place with all the importance of an event in her young life. With it sentiment came to the front. Philosophy and reason retreated. Manon lost herself in dreams of "the raptures of love, the beauty of filial affection, the peace of domestic life, and the joys of motherhood."

Naturally enough, Manon's first sign of her appreciation of Rousseau was an attempt to find a Saint-Preux to whom she might play the part of Julie. She looked in vain for such a one among the host of tradesmen lovers whom her father favored. They were all of them stupid. They could talk of nothing more inspiring than the gossip of the Pont Neuf. Manon could not give forth the faintest spark for one of them. The

idea of choosing a Saint-Preux from among them
was quite preposterous.

However, there chanced to be a lover for Manon,
a possible Saint-Preux outside this tradesmen-
throng. He wrote verses and he had theories,
and he could talk of something other than the
gossip of the Pont Neuf, so wearisome to Manon.
He was a semi-philosopher, semi-sentimentalist.
His name was La Blancherie.

There is mention of La Blancherie early in
Manon's letters, before her mother's death. The
young man, it seems, had met Manon at one of
those gatherings of *belle esprits* which she occasionally attended. He had devoted himself to her,
had captured her young fancy, and obtained per-
mission from her to call upon her. Manon had
received his attentions with some pride and pleasure. She had not jested about him as about her
other lovers. She had regarded him as a young
sage, a future Rousseau possibly. She had become,
indeed, quite enthusiastic on his account. Her
hitherto frigid little heart had warmed, had glowed
and burned for him. The fire that La Blancherie
had kindled was not love, perhaps, and yet surely
it was something more ardent than admiration.
Of course, Manon had confided to Sophie this
solemn event in her interior life. Without her
mother's knowledge, she had added postscripts to
the letters bound for Amiens. She had been very
serious, very reverent in her treatment of this new,

sweet, and inexpressibly mysterious sentiment.
As for La Blancherie, he had not been slow. He
had seen "papa," had proposed for Manon's hand,
and had been rejected by monsieur, because of his
lack of financial resource. Therewith, he had left
Paris and had gone to Amiens, supposedly to build
up the necessary fortune.

Such was the standing of the La Blancherie affair
at the time of Madame Phlipon's death. Some
months after this event, so sorrowful for Manon,
La Blancherie returned to Paris. He called upon
Manon and appeared to be much affected by her
pale and sad appearance. Manon tremulously
spoke to him of her grief. He sought to comfort
her and showed her the proof sheets of his new
book. Manon wrote to Sophie of the book, that
it was her "whole soul," and of the author she said
that she could not judge him because he was so
much "like" herself. She had persuaded herself
that she was in love, that La Blancherie was the
Saint-Preux for whom she had been waiting.

Monsieur Phlipon, however, proved recalcitrant.
He did not find that La Blancherie had in any
way bettered his financial condition. He disapproved of the young man and requested that he
abate his visits. This paternal mandate was the
needed incentive to Manon's love. Distance, in
her case, certainly lent enchantment. Separated
from her Saint-Preux, her romantic young brain
seethed and bubbled amazingly. She idealized the

young man into a being of talent and integrity
quite different from what he really was. As a
matter of fact, La Blancherie was very ordinary,
his verses and his theories were "twaddle," his
philosophy and his sentiment were second-rate.
It was only by means of a most superficial acquaintance that he had succeeded with Manon.

Manon awoke from her love's young dream
when, one day, walking in the Luxembourg, she
met her lover with a feather in his hat. This
frivolous ornament, a mere trifle to be sure (but
to a woman's mind trifles sometimes assume vast
proportions), shocked and revolted Manon. Immediately the young man was a changed being in
her eyes. "His features," she wrote to Sophie,
"though the same, have no longer the same expression and do not indicate the same qualities.
Oh, how powerful is illusion! He is no more an
idol of perfection, no longer the first of his species,
— in short, no longer my beloved."

This episode of the feather, together with some
idle gossip which she heard to the effect that La
Blancherie was commonly known as "the lover of
the eleven thousand virgins," quite cured Manon
of her temporary derangement. She granted the
young man one last interview in which she took
occasion to inform him that he was not the paragon
she had once supposed him, but a very average
mortal, with whom she could have no concern.
La Blancherie, a bit chagrined and looking very

foolish, took up his hat and withdrew. When the door closed behind him, it shut him out forever from the life of Mademoiselle Phlipon. Manon's first love affair was over.

From love Manon turned to friendship with redoubled fervor. Sophie alone could not suffice her. Henriette, Sophie's older sister, of whom Manon had disapproved in her convent days, came to Paris on a visit. Her vivacity and wit charmed Manon. She was admitted as a third to the intimacy. Thenceforth the letters to Amiens were addressed to both sisters. The truth was, Manon had grown a little away from Sophie and nearer to Henriette. Sophie still inhabited a world of mysticism and piety and even meditated taking the veil. Manon had departed from that world into a wider circle — the circle in which Henriette had always resided. Under such circumstances it was inevitable that the alliance should become a triple one. The correspondence had lost its unity. And so, too, had Manon's life. At this period Manon was living in a way that might justly be described as "scrappy, patchy, and unfulfilled." She was deep in domestic troubles. Her father was leading an irregular life. His fortune was fast vanishing. Ruin seemed imminent. "I shall have great need of philosophy to enable me to sustain the conflicts that are coming," wrote Manon to her Amiens friends. "I am like Ulysses clinging to the fig tree; I wait for the ebb tide to restore me to my ship."

When she wrote thus Manon was twenty-two
years of age. Her sorrow at her mother's death,
her little love affair, her household cares and
worries had developed and matured her. She was
a girl of very exceptional mind and charapter. It
was not surprising that she should have attracted
the attention of men of mark. Better than the
society of young men she enjoyed that of the older
men, distinguished by experience and culture, who
came to see her.

Her Memoirs and her letters have much to say
of a certain Monsieur de Sainte-Lette. He was
about sixty years of age, a man who had travelled
much, who had done government service in
Louisiana, and who had recently come to Paris
from Pondicherry. Manon and he became great
chums. Of this friendship Manon wrote: "There
is perfect freedom between us. We talk on all
sorts of subjects. I question him, I listen, I reflect, I object; when we do not wish to talk we
keep silent without troubling ourselves, but that
does not last long. Sometimes we read a fragment
suggested by our conversation, something well
known and classic, whose beauties we love to
review. The last was a song of the poet Rousseau
and some verses by Voltaire."

Sainte-Lette had a widower friend, Monsieur de
Sevelinges, a man of some fifty odd years of age,
who held a position in the finances of the province
and cultivated letters as well. Through Sainte-

Lette, Manon became acquainted with Sevelinges. With Sevelinges as with Sainte-Lette she reasoned, philosophized, and rhapsodized. Moreover, she spoke to him of her domestic troubles. He condoned with her and on his part confided to her his regrets on the score of his lonely widowerhood. Sentimental passages ensued between them. There was even talk of marriage. However, the affair came to nothing. Sevelinges went away and Manon gradually ceased to think of him, as she became much interested in another philosopher friend.

This other philosopher friend was Monsieur Roland de la Platierre. He was a friend of the sisters Cannet and much revered by them. Indeed, between him and Henriette there had been at one time some sort of a sentimental attachment. Monsieur Roland was an inspector of commerce in Picardy and lived at Amiens. In his business capacity he went often to Paris. Naturally enough he had heard much of Manon from the Cannets and had become acquainted with her portrait as it hung in the Cannet home.

One day he remarked to the Amiens girls, "I am about to set out for Paris. Why not give me the opportunity of knowing this dear friend of yours, Mademoiselle Phlipon? Will you not entrust me with a letter to her?"

The letter was written and Roland was appointed its carrier. Of course as a messenger from the beloved Sophie he was well received.

" An enlightened man of pure morals who can be
reproached with nothing save his preference for the
ancients over the moderns and his foible of being
somewhat overfond of talking of himself,"— it
was thus Sophie's letter described the man who
delivered it.   Manon raised her eyes from the
written words and contemplated her new visitor.
She saw a rather austere looking gentleman of
more than forty years of age.   His face was
long and thin, his hair certainly not overbundant,
his features regular, his manners stiff, and his
dress conspicuous in its simplicity.   Clearly he
was not at all a handsome man, but he had a subtle
and very pleasing smile, an air of piquancy, and
an appearance that was on the whole imposing and
distinguished.   All this Manon noted as she looked
at him.   Later, as she talked with him, she was
impressed with his knowledge, his good sense, and
his excellent taste.

Such was Manon's first acquaintance with the
man destined to play so important a part in her
life.   During his stay in Paris she did not see him
very often.   He was much occupied with business.
But there were occasional " visits " which extended
to a late hour in the evening.   Manon and Roland
found much to talk to each other about.   He told
her of his business and his travels.   She asked
him questions in regard to the Italian which she
was studying.   They discussed literature.   They
were a pair of sage philosophers together.

However, there must have been, even at this early date in their acquaintance, some romance mixed with the philosophy; for when the moment came for Roland to bid his fair young friend good-bye, he asked for something which we are not accustomed to associate with Plato and the others of his school. Manon, it seems, complied with his request, and not without the accompanying blush.

Sainte-Lette happened to be standing near. There appears to have been a truly French freedom about the whole transaction.

" You are fortunate in departing," the older man remarked, dryly. " Make haste to return in order to obtain another."

Roland left Paris on a journey that took him to Switzerland, Italy, Sicily, and Malta. He studied the industries of these countries and took notes upon them. By previous arrangement, he sent his notes to Manon to preserve for him. Manon became much interested in his travels and investigation as related by himself. She came to admire more and more the man's clear, intelligent, and methodic mind.

On the completion of his journey Roland returned home by way of Paris. Yet even at this period Manon did not see him very regularly. He was a cautious gentleman. He understood Manon and knew that she was not to be won by precipitation. He moved with the slowness and sureness of fate itself. Manon pretended to be much piqued by

his wariness. She wrote to the Amiens friends
that Monsieur Roland appeared to her " through too
long a telescope," that for all she saw of him he
might as well have remained in Italy. There is
some artifice in this. Manon, who had always been
so frank, was reticent on the subject of this mutual
friend. The truth was Roland did not wish to have
the Cannet sisters know that he saw Manon often.
He feared gossip and then, too, he apprehended that
Henriette, who had once liked him in something
more than a moderate degree, might be jealous.

The affair between Manon and Roland advanced
secretly along Platonic lines. Roland, however, at
length became ardent. He did not feel sure of
Manon. He wished to meet her on a more
subtanstial footing than the dream basis over which,
for so long a while, they had been pleasantly drift-
ing. He told her that he loved her and asked her
to become his wife.

Manon answered in pretty platitudes, but would
give him no direct answer. She told him, in very
impersonal fashion, that she was not a good enough
match for him. She disclosed to him the facts of
her ruined fortune and of her father's irregular
life. Roland, however, persisted. At length it
was agreed that he should write a letter to Monsieur Phlipon asking for Manon's hand.

Roland returned to Amiens and wrote the letter
from there. Monsieur Phlipon answered in very
impertinent and bumptious fashion. He did not

like Monsieur Roland. The man's air of conscious virtue and superiority angered him. He did not want him for a son-in-law and did not hesitate to tell Monsieur Roland so. He showed a copy of his answer to Manon.

Manon was very much mortified and indignant when she saw what her father had written. He and she had been growing farther and farther apart. He was proud of her, but he disliked the philosophy that made her refuse some rich husband of his own choosing. Moreover, he saw that she considered herself better than him, and this annoyed him. As for Manon, she was not, perhaps, as tender and patient as she might have been. She doubtless showed too plainly her disapproval of his loose conduct. And the tone she took towards him may have been a little too censorious. At any rate there was constant friction between them. Manon felt that this must end, that the moment of crisis had come, that she must act. Her father's letter to Roland determined her. She took matters into her own hands, left her father for good, and retired to an apartment in the convent of the Congregation. There she lived economically, quietly, studiously.

When Manon went to the convent, she wrote to Roland that all thought of an engagement between them must be banished. Henceforth they could be only friends. Perplexed, aggrieved, well nigh distracted, Roland acquiesced. He wrote heartbroken letters to Manon, and she answered in the same mournful vein. They were both very miserable over their separation.

The affair was at this distressing standstill when at length Roland arrived in Paris. He called upon Manon at the convent. He went to scold, but the sight of her beautiful, sad face, the tears that were in her eyes as she regarded him, quite vanquished him. He remained only to love. He took the dear, unkind, unreasonable girl in his arms and once more implored her to marry him.

"Is it yes or no, Manon?" he inquired.

It was yes. Manon could no longer resist the call of this wise, learned, and upright man, the call of marriage, of domestic life, of love. Her feeling for Roland was a romantic friendship in which philosophy and sentiment blended. She believed she could be happy with him. With her clear vision she looked before her and saw new cares, new responsibilities, new experiences. She went forward to meet them, firmly, courageously, as at a later day she went to meet her last great crisis.

Manon's girlhood is at an end. On the eve of her marriage it has become a thing apart, a picture, a memory. It is in retrospect only a humble first act. Yet what a remarkable first act! The recollection of its purity, its vigor, its activity remains after the knowledge of other grander, more pretentious scenes is past. There is in it inspiration and the health and beneficence that are in all good things.

II.

IT was afternoon. The session of the Assembly
was at an end. The meeting of the Jacobins had
not yet opened. A band of patriots were gathered
in a pleasant salon of the Hotel Britannique. They
argued, they wavered, they compromised. They
were carried this way and that with the ebb and
flow of political debate.

Viewed even as they were then, at an early period
in the Revolution, before the light of subsequent
events had irradiated them, they were an interesting
group of men. He of the ruddy cheeks and honest
countenance was Petion, soon to be chosen mayor
of Paris. Near by was one who said very little, but
who heard all, a neatly dressed, sallow faced man.
This man was Robespierre. There, too, was Brissot,
the republican journalist, distinguished by his
gaiety, his naïveté, his boyishness, his frank and
winning smile. The austere gentleman, the Cato
of the throng, was Roland. And there beside him,
young, handsome, grave, the most lofty and daring
spirit of them all was Buzot. There were others besides these foremost ones, Clavière, Louis Noailles,
Volfius, and Garran. Together they discussed the

affairs of the Assembly, criticised its dilatoriness, and suggested measures that should be taken to advance the interests of the people.

In the same salon with them, near a window and before a little table, a woman was seated writing. She was the wife of one of the number, of Roland, the host of the salon. In her capacity of hostess, she rose to receive each man as he came and to exchange some few pleasant amenities with him before he left. For the rest, she took no part in the conversation. Apparently her whole attention was given to her writing. Yet, at every expression of a high minded sentiment, her eyes flashed and her color deepened, and at an ill-timed jest or a foolish argument she bit her lips and her pen sputtered in protest.

"Oh, these Frenchmen," she was thinking. "They do not know how to deliberate. A certain lightness leads them from one subject to another. Their attention is easily fatigued. A laugh is awakened by a word, and a jest overthrows logic. Why will they not see that it is impossible to do good in politics save by combined effort, that unless each one is willing to bend to an idea a little different from his own, there can be no united action and nothing will be accomplished?"

The voices of the men grew loud in disagreement. Madame's pen went sputtering on its way.

Clavière, who happened to be standing nearest to madame, glanced down at her, remarking com-

passionately, " How rapidly you write — and in
this furor! Only a woman's head is capable of
such a thing."

Madame looked up, smiling. " What would you
say," she asked, " if I should repeat all your arguments?"

The gentlemen were leaving. One by one they
stopped beside madame's chair to exchange a few
words with her before departing. At length there
remained only Brissot, Robespierre, Petion, Buzot,
and Roland. These latter gentlemen, left alone,
turned to Madame Roland, anxious for her
opinion.

" Well, what do you think of to-day's business?"
they inquired. " Do we go backward like the
crab or slowly forward like the turtle?" This
was said part in jest and in appreciation of the
woman's swift, eager spirit.

Madame Roland pushed back her papers and
rose from her table. Impetuously, a bit scornfully,
determinedly she faced the men. " You are nothing but children," she exclaimed. " Your enthusiasm is a momentary blaze. A civil war is
necessary before you will be worth anything.' 'Tis
blood we want, since nothing else will whip you
and make you go. War! war! We must beat to
battle or retreat. There is no middle course."

Something like the joy of battle thrilled in
madame's voice and shone in her eyes. She was
terrible in her cruelty. But in her cruelty, its

cause, its very essence, was the divine spark. Her wrath was " the wrath of the gods," her indignation the " righteous indignation " of the moralist. Her call for " blood " was in accordance with that " divine right of insurrection " which she preached, a means towards that "complete regeneration " which she most rigorously demanded.

To the patriots whom she addressed Madame Roland's words were now as always fresh incentive, renewed inspiration. She was in " the vanguard " of their movement. They looked to her as to " the watcher on the ramparts " urging them to the fight. We can imagine their listening attention. If there was one among them who held back and said nothing, that one, we may be sure, was Robespierre. Perhaps in his politic soul even so soon he had begun to cherish a contempt for Madame Roland's uncalculating daring and indifference to consequence. Already a dark thought, like the shadow of the guillotine, may have traversed his mind. If there was another whose eyes flashed with a fire like her own, who stood beside her on the ramparts in the forefront of the fray, that other, we may know, was Buzot. Perhaps, even at that early date, the fire of his glance may have contained the spark of love. Already similar hopes and dreams and aspirations may have been drawing him to her, uniting his soul to her soul with the inevitableness of fate.

But though one may have hung back ominously

and another have pressed forward too fervently,
all were stirred, all were incited in one way or
another by her words. Madame Roland, it is
certain, had acquired at this period " a veritable
supremacy " over these men and over all the
patriots of her acquaintance. And this is not surprising. All reasons, save that of her sex, made
her their natural leader. She was the most determined, the most inspired of them all. She
never wavered when they wavered, or stopped at
practical considerations when they stopped. She
was uncompromising, unswerving, unalterable in
her purpose. She gave herself exclusively to the
cause ; she would not go to the theatre or look at
pictures or do anything for the mere gratification
of her tastes. " Who is the traitor," she demanded, " who has other interest to-day than that
of the nation ? " Triumphant in her hopefulness,
she pictured a future made glorious by the realization of an ideal government. With " an almost
clairvoyant vision," she looked into the future and
foretold what would be the needs, what the responsibilities of this government. Her stand was
the firmest, her loyalty the surest, her aspirations
the highest, her sight the clearest. She embodied
in their purest form the principles of the patriot
cause.

This woman to whom all eyes turned as to " the
type and symbol of the Republic " was one with
the young girl who had sighed for the time of the

saints and the heroes, whose eyes had filled with
tears in contemplation of the beauty and solemnity
of the universe. In essence, the real essence, that
is of the soul, Madame Roland was still Manon
Phlipon, responsive, idealistic, incorruptible.

Manon's life since her marriage, to the time when
the beginnings of the Revolution were shaking
France, had been quiet, industrious, intensely
domestic. Manon had married Roland on Feb. 4,
1784, when her twenty-sixth birthday was close at
hand. She and her husband had lived first at
Paris and then at Amiens. Since 1784, and until
the Revolution of '89, they had been established in
the district of Lyons, dividing their time between
the city and the neighboring town of Villefranche
and Roland's ancestral home, the close of La Plâtière, situated near the village of Thézée, in the
midst of the beautiful Beaujolais woods and mountains.

The young wife constituted herself her husband's assistant in his industrial and economic
labors. She was his proofreader, his copyist, his
editor. She devoted herself to him with irreproach-
able tact and gentleness and submission. She made
herself indispensable to him.

In the second year of her marriage her child was
born, a daughter, to whom was given the name
Eudora. Madame Roland, true to the teachings
of her revered Rousseau, did not, according to the
fashion prevalent among mothers of the time, put

her baby out to nurse, but herself took entire charge
of the little one. Eudora, it must be confessed,
was something of a trial to her mother. As she
grew into a healthy, hearty child, it became manifest that she was more frolicsome than studious,
that she loved her doll better than her Plutarch.
Her mother in despair betook herself to Rousseau
and sought to learn from Emile and Julie the way
to imbue her daughter with the proper sentiment
and enthusiasm.

During the years before the Revolution, Madame Roland's happiest times were passed at the
close of La Plâtière. In a spirit of rapturous an-
ticipation she had approached her home among the
hills. It was to be her Clarens. Rousseau had
painted for her in glowing colors that ideal country existence, those delightful meditations, those
wholesome, hearty duties. And the reality did not
fall far short of the dream. Life at the close was
made easy and pleasant for her by her activity, her
industry, her firm hold on homely, every day con-
cerns. Within doors she kept the accounts and
directed the servants. Out of doors she superintended the toil of the vine-dresser, the gathering-in
of the harvest, the affairs of the poultry yard. She
appreciated, she loved all these details of domestic
and rural simplicity.

In addition to her duties about the house and on
the farm, Madame Roland undertook the care of
her neighbors, the peasants of Thézée. When oc-

casion demanded she nursed them, she helped them, she comforted them. Their welfare was among her chief considerations. She endeared herself to the peasants, and one of her last thoughts was of them and of her pride and happiness in the consciousness of their love.

Life at the close afforded ample scope for the affections. Friends came often and stayed long. A delightful hospitality was maintained. Then there was always the little Eudora who, wonderful to relate, was improving under her mother's Rousseau-flavored doctrines. And there was always Roland. During these years Madame Roland had not abated her labors as her husband's assistant. She continued to copy, to read proof, to polish and revise for him. She and Roland were very happy together. He was more in love with his beautiful, clever young wife than ever. And as for madame, she loved him as a daughter loves a father. She continued always to revere in him the wisdom, integrity, and austerity which had first attracted her to him. She knew no higher, better companionship than this with him, and it satisfied her.

On the whole, Madame Roland was well off. She might have gone on in this way busily, pleasantly, quietly to the end. Had it not been for an unusual stress of circumstances, she might have remained content in her obscurity, without a thought of broader aims and larger possibilities. But elements of dissolution were at work. Clouds were gathering which were to break in a fierce tempest over France. The Revolution was at hand and in its tumultuous rush of thought and action Madame Roland was caught up and carried far away from her vines, her chickens, and her peasants, and her obscure fireside happiness.

Madame Roland and her husband were among those who enthusiastically welcomed the Revolution of '89. Their responsive souls had felt the rage and sufferings of the people. They had burned to ameliorate the people's wrongs. At first all that they desired was reform. The country was to be rid of its ancient abuses. Those taxes that "so piteously ravaged town and province," those restrictions that so "crippled" industries and manufactures were to be abolished. The old régime was to pass away, and in its place was to rise a new government founded upon justice and a liberal constitution. Hopefully they turned their eyes to the Assembly that met on May 4, at Versailles. Industriously, earnestly, they went to work upon the cahiers, memorials setting forth the people's grievances, that were to go from Lyons to the Assembly at Versailles.

During the days between May 4 and July 14, from their quiet home among the Beaujolais they watched the proceedings of the Assembly. What they viewed there did not satisfy them. They grew suspicious of the new administrative body. They criticised and condemned it.

In the storming of the Bastile, on July 14, Madame Roland saw the rising of the rightful and long repressed " sovereign." It was for her the dawning of a new and very beautiful ideal. She no longer asked for reform. It was complete regeneration that she demanded. Henceforth she spurned all palliative measures. She put no faith in the promises of the king. For the half-way course of the constitutional party she had only contempt and loathing. It was of revolution that she talked, revolution and the foundation of a republic. She turned her eyes to Greece and Rome and America, to the liberty that had blessed these countries, to the words and actions of their heroes. She dreamed of establishing a free government in France.

Madame Roland's political views were lofty, but they were human and, as such, subject to error and excess. She shared the fault of her time in suspecting and condemning all who did not think as she thought. All who were not so swift, so impatient as herself, she stigmatized as intriguers and traitors to the cause. She was fierce, passionate, bitter in her denunciation. It is especially hard to forgive her strictures on the revered La Fayette. She herself afterwards softened these strictures. She came to regard the general's reactionary attitude as an early revolt against that " overweening popular ascendency" which she turned and faced when it was too late.

Moreover, Madame Roland was not always practical. She was a moralist, a theorist, an idealist. She thought deeply and broadly. She argued eloquently. But when it was a question of definite ends and aims, she sometimes fell into the error of " vagueness and insufficiency." Yet in spite of occasional lapses, her sense was, on the whole, sound, her judgments keen and lucid.

Early in the Revolution the Rolands put themselves in touch with certain sympathetic spirits. They became especially intimate with Brissot who was editing " Le Patriote Français." Roland and madame, both of them, contributed to his journal and corresponded with him. They also were in communication with Champagneux, who had started in Lyons " Le Courrier de Lyon," similar in character to Brissot's journal. They wrote often for this paper. Moreover, the Rolands were on very friendly terms with Bosc, a young scientist, whom they had known ever since the first year of their marriage, and with Lanthenas, a doctor, who had long been a frequent and welcome visitor in their home. Madame wrote patriotic letters to both of these men who were in Paris in the heart of affairs. She was forever inciting them to action. She also corresponded in very spirited vein with a young lawyer, Bancal des Issarts, whom Lanthenas had introduced to her and her husband. Thus by correspondence and by frequent contributions to the political journals of the day, Madame Roland did all in her power to urge on the patriot cause.

At length the time came when she was able to take a more active part. The municipality of Lyons was sending deputies to Paris to claim from the Assembly the payment of the debt which the old régime had forced upon the city. Roland was one of the deputies chosen to go. He went, and madame went with him.

During their stay in Paris, a period of a few months, from February, 1791, to September of the same year, the Rolands resided on the Rue Guéné-gaud in the Hotel Britanique. There, in their pleasant salon, they received, as we have seen, the leaders of the patriot cause.

The Assembly sat only a short distance away in the Manège of the Tuileries. Thither madame repaired and sat in judgment on the body. Its waverings exasperated and finally angered her. She found the leaders of '89, the " impartials " as they were called, the most dangerous enemies of the Revolution. In April she left the Assembly in wrath, not to revisit it during her stay.

She turned her attention to the patriot clubs. These she attended with her husband and sent letters to some of them. She would not sign her letters, however. She believed that under exist-ing customs women should work quietly, not con-spicuously ; they should inspire and inflame, but take no public part.

Such being her opinion, she governed her actions
in accordance always. Even in her own salon at the
gathering of patriots she remained, as we know,
seated at her little table. Sometimes it was a
book that occupied her, sometimes it was her
needlework, but oftenest it was her writing. To
the casual observer she appeared uninterested, a
person of no consequence in the debate. Yet by
many of those assembled there, by all who knew
her intimately, her presence was never for a
moment forgotten. They realized her keen interest, her constant attention, and took both into
account. Unconsciously, involuntarily almost,
they appealed to her. She was silently invoked,
tacitly addressed. Truly she was in all of these
meetings the controlling influence, the real power.

Over these meetings of the patriots, as over the
sittings of the Assembly, Madame Roland sat in
judgment. She was full of enthusiasm for the
high-mindedness, the courage, the eloquence of her
friends, but she was not blind to their faults. She
lamented their lightness, their vagaries of speech,
their lack of unity, their impatience with one
another.

With her keen and virile intellect she comprehended the weakness of the movement which she
was urging on. She saw how very distant was the
goal of her aspirations. She and her patriot friends
she realized were in the case of that "forlorn hope
which must needs fight and conquer for the army."

But her determination never faltered. It was for " the happiness of future generations " that she pressed boldly on. With her clear, discerning vision she perceived the clouds ahead. " I know that good citizens such as I see every day regard the future with tranquil eyes," she said, " but I am more than ever convinced that they are deluded." However, it was for the sun beyond the clouds that she worked and waited. " I shall die when it may please heaven," she declared, " but my last breath will be an aspiration of joy and hope for coming generations."

That which troubled Madame Roland more than the weakness of her friends, more even than what seemed to her the perfidy of the Assembly, was the indifferent attitude of the people. They were not bent on revolution. They were not dreaming of a republic. Since their storming of the Bastile, which had so rejoiced and inspired Madame Roland, they had subsided, so madame considered, into " lethargy." They had fallen back into " the sleep of the enslaved." The public conscience was dormant. To awaken this conscience, to arouse the people to a realization of their " sovereign " rights, she was ready to welcome any excesses. She exulted over the flight of the king on June 22. She regarded it as a virtual abdication. The duty of the country now, she determined, was to declare Louis XVI. dethroned and so establish a republic. She lamented his capture. " But for this," she thought, "civil war would have been inevitable and the nation would have been forced into the grand school of public virtues." She and her friends desired the trial of the king. To bring this about they united with demagogues and agitators, the mob element of the streets. In consequence of this alliance came the events of the Champ-de-Mars on July 17. Madame Roland joined with those who called these events a "massacre." She was exasperated. She despaired of ever seeing her ideals realized. The public mind, she determined, was incapable of anything lofty and daring.

Monsieur Roland's business was at an end. Madame was glad to leave Paris, its "dolts" and its "knaves," and retire with her husband to their retreat among the Beaujolais hills. At least she thought for a time that she was glad. In reality her interest in public events was so vigorous, her devotion to the cause so intense, that she stifled under the nullity of her provincial home. She knew that there were heights to be climbed and battles to be fought. Her eyes were lifted to those heights, her warrior blood coursed in her veins. She could not rest content cultivating her lettuce, sitting with her needle-work at her obscure fireside, while there was a chance that, by being in the centre of affairs, she might help in that great work that sooner or later must be accomplished or the patriot cause be lost forever.

Could Madame Roland have foreseen her own prominent and tragic part in that great work, we may be sure she would not for one moment have halted. Her acquaintance with the philosophers and the noble minds of antiquity had taught her a certain contempt for all personal considerations, all selfish happiness. She was ready, more than that, she was eager to sacrifice all to the goal of humanity. Truly she was in spirit very like those large-souled Roman matrons, Cornelia and the rest, of whom she loved to read. She was compounded of heroic stuff, her level was a high one; and this she yearned to prove.

It was decided that the little Eudora needed to become acquainted with the sights of Paris, that Roland could perform his work, which was the encyclopedia, better in the capital, among savants and artists, than at " the bottom of a desert," for so the home at the close had come to be regarded. Accordingly, in December the Rolands went up to Paris.

When the Rolands arrived in Paris the new Assembly, called the legislative to distinguish it from its successor, the constituent, was in session. Among its members were a group of young and ardent enthusiasts known as the Girond, the name of the department from which many of them had come. Like Madame Roland, these young men from an early age had nourished their minds on Plutarch and Rousseau. They spoke in classic

phrase, they thought high thoughts, dreamed
beautiful dreams. They believed implicitly in
their ideals and their own power to accomplish
their ideals. They considered themselves charged
with the regeneration of France, the dissemination
of liberty, the foundation of a republic. They
regarded themselves as the saviours, the " Providence" of their country.

Allied with the Girondists were the Rolands'
old friends, Brissot and Petion, both high in
power. Brissot was conspicuous in the Assembly,
a deputy from Paris, and Petion was mayor of
Paris.

To the aid of Brissot, Petion, and the Girondists,
the Rolands brought their own bright hopes and
daring projects. Madame Roland felt her affinity
to these Plutarchian heroes, these so many Solons
and Brutuses and Phocions, as they loved to call
themselves. Her husband was Cato and she was
Cato's wife, and these others were their companion
spirits with whom they were to join in raising a
fair Utopia.

The beauty of all this republican rhapsodizing
was its sincerity. To be sure, it was tinged, in
Madame Roland's case at least, with a certain
bourgeois jealousy and vanity. She shared the
sentiments of the class from which she came — the
third estate. She resented the superiority of
birth, the advantages of material splendor, the
social slights that she had been made to endure

because of her own humble condition. She looked
forward to a new order of things in which virtue
and talent were to be the standards. And she had
a presentiment that nowhere were these standards
to be found in such perfection as in her own little
circle, in the persons of herself, her husband, and
their youthful, Plutarchian companions. Such
self-complacency is perhaps amusing. We cannot
wonder that some adverse critics have seen fit to
satirize it. And yet it came of an honest and just
enthusiasm. We may smile at Madame Roland
and her friends, but we smile indulgently. It is
impossible not to love that inspiring group of
patriots whose tragic fate has irradiated them.
We forget their short-comings in the thought of
their triumphant constancy and courage.

Brief pen portraits of the foremost of the Girond,
done with Madame Roland's distinct and vivid
touch, have come down to us. We are permitted
to see these men in action, confidentially, in the
privacy of the Roland's salon. There are the impetuous Gaudet, the two deliberate Gensenné, and
Vergniaud, the poet orator, whose downcast eyes
that "could so lighten under the magic power of
speech" madame "distrusted," she knew not
"wherefore." In vain she searched among them
for one able and powerful enough to be their
leader. Each was lacking in some essential point.
Even when she urged Brissot to assume command,
she did so doubtingly, believing him to be "exces-

sively hopeful and of a pliant and even guileless
nature." Her husband she knew to be too inflex-
ible for all practical purposes. He with his thin
white hair plastered stiffly down, his sombre dress,
and his buckleless shoes contributed to that youthful group the dignity and austerity of age.
Madame Roland, it was said, might have passed
for his daughter, so fresh and brilliant was her
complexion, so singularly youthful her air of
blended candor and reserve. She it was who was
called the "soul" of the Girond. She inspired,
she inflamed, she encouraged with unceasing
energy. Could she, it has been asked, had she
been a man, have acted as the captain of the band,
have led them on to victory? Some of her
admirers like to think so.

Arrived in Paris, the Rolands established themselves in the Rue de la Harpe. There they lived
quietly for a few months. In March, through the
influence of Brissot and other Girondists who at
that time were controlling the Assembly, Roland
was appointed to the Council of the King as
Minister of the Interior.

The new office produced no change in the
Rolands' mode of living. While residing officially
in an "elegant building" of Calonne's arrangement, the Hotel of the Interior, they retained their
apartment in the Rue de la Harpe. Madame
Roland neither made nor received visits. She
entertained only the members of the ministry and

such deputies and political personages as Roland desired to see. Roland persisted in his sombre style of dress. The court elevated its eyebrows at the ribbon bows upon his shoes. He resembled a Quaker in Sunday costume, it declared. One who saw the family at this period described the minister's austere looks, madame's freshness, simplicity, and youthfulness of appearance, and the child who "capered round with hair rippling to her waist." "You would have said," declared the narrator, "that they were inhabitants of Pennsylvania transplanted to the salon of Monsieur de Calonne."

It has truly been stated that Madame Roland "entered the ministry with her husband." She had made herself, as we know, indispensable to him in his literary work during the first year of their marriage. She had never resigned her office of assistant and adviser. Now she went over his mail with him every day, discussed with him the affairs of his office, and helped him to decide the course to be pursued. Many people, realizing her influence, went to her with their business before interviewing Roland.

The questions which, at the time of Roland's ministry, were agitating the Assembly were the edicts against the non-conformist priests and the emigrés. The king put his veto to these measures. Thus, so Madame Roland maintained, he gave proof of his insincerity. At length she persuaded

Roland and Sevran, Minister of War, that Louis was not to be trusted. During these days France was in a bad way. Religious troubles were flaming up everywhere. A contra-revolution led by the recalcitrant priests was feared. In April war against the Austrians was declared. Rumor had it that treachery was rife, that the king, the court party, and the officers of the army were plotting to receive the enemy, to massacre the patriots, and to restore the old régime.

Two measures Madame Roland recommended as cures for all the evils with which the country was visited: in the first place, that there should be a proscription of all the non-conformist priests; in the second place, that a camp of twenty thousand soldiers should be convoked to guard the city. In a spirit of patriotic exaltation she seated herself beside her table and wrote, under cover of her husband's name, a letter to the king, urging his consent to the two measures.

Louis refused to give his sanction. Exasperated by the pressure put upon him by Roland and the other Girond ministers, he dismissed them.

The Rolands left the Hotel of the Interior and retired to their little apartment in the Rue de la Harpe. This moment of their removal was one of the proudest in Madame Roland's life. Her letter was being read and applauded in the Assembly. She believed that it would convince the country of Louis's treachery, that it would lead to

a recall of the Girondist ministers, the deposition
of the king, and the establishment of a republic.
She thought that she had performed her mission of
" usefulness and glory."

Madame's mind, however, was swifter than that
of the public.   The populace, it is true, assembled,
armed, and visited the Assembly and the palace of
the king, crying : " Sanction the decrees.   Restore
the patriot ministers."   But there was no mention
of deposition or a republic.   The events of June 20,
to all appearances, were nothing more than an
unusually tumultuous Mardi-gras.

Reaction followed.   The constitutionalists rallied
for a desperate stand.   The court plotted with the
allies and the emigrés across the border to strike a
blow that should shatter this new and formidable
régime.

In the face of such opposition, the patriots redoubled their efforts.   From their seats in the
Assembly the Girondist leaders made public decla-
ration that the country was in   danger.   They
called upon the departments everywhere and the
sections of Paris to act.   There was an immediate
response.   Troops began to collect from all over
France.   Old men and boys, even women and
girls, answered the call. France offered its very life.

At first the popular movement was directed only
against the foreign foe.   But, as the days went on,
guided by the wills of its abettors, Robespierre
in control of the Jacobin Club, Danton, and Marat,

it changed its course. The king's throne became
its goal. It advanced with a swiftness and a fury
that alarmed the more moderate minds. Many of
the Girondists, among them Brissot, Vergniaud,
Gaudet, and Gensenné, drew back and sought to
calm the passionate forces they had roused. Madame
Roland, however, pressed on undaunted. It was
the court party, the aristocrats, whom she feared,
not the people of France. To her the people were
still a divine element, a means by which the salva-
tion of the country was to be attained. With the
aid of her husband and Barbaroux, a young
patriot from the south, she urged on the insurrection.

On August 10 that which she had so fervently and so unceasingly desired happened. The
people became the "sovereign." A great mob
surged through the city and into the hall of the
Assembly. In accordance with the will of the
new "sovereign," the Assembly, composed only of
its Girondist and Jacobin members, voted the
suspension of the king, restored the patriot ministers to office, and summoned a national convention to
decide on a future free government for France.
Monarchy had fallen in a day. For Madame
Roland it was a day of triumph. She believed
that her republic was at hand.

She was soon to be disillusioned, however. In
a very little while she was to discover that the
people were not that divinity she had imagined

them, that France was not "fit" for the republic of
which she had dreamed.

For a time all went well. But it was not long
before her husband, restored to the ministry, found
himself opposed by an insurrectionary element
among the patriots, a fierce, vindictive, blood-
thirsty element. When he gave commands, they
were disregarded. To be sure, he represented the
law, it was conceded; but were not the people
superior to the law, it was demanded. Were they
not the "saviours" of their country, the "sovereign" power of France? When, in horror, he
recoiled from the rule of terror, the general proscription, and the September massacres, he was
branded as a traitor and accused of being in league
with the court party, and of conspiring against
the unity and indivisibility of the republic.

The position of Roland and of Madame Roland,
and of all the sincere Girondists, was difficult and
sad. They had pressed on bravely, hopefully, fervently, only to find "a river of blood" flowing at
their feet. In humanity, in conscience, they could
not cross to the other side with Danton, Marat,
Robespierre, and the others. They must remain
where they were and take their stand, perilous
and desperate though it was, against the mad
onrush of anarchy.

They clung to their dream so long as it was
possible, believing it too "beautiful" to abandon.
But at length that had to go with the rest, the lost
power, the lost hopes, and the lost friends.

Madame Roland's awakening was terrible. When she had rhapsodized about the divine right of insurrection, she had done so unknowingly. All along her enthusiasm had been the enthusiasm of the inexperienced idealist. Now she was brought face to face with the facts, she saw the people armed with pikes, organized into brigades, volcanic and brutal. The reality sickened her. "You know my enthusiasm for the Revolution," she wrote. "Well, I am ashamed of it. It is stained by these wretches. It has become hideous. It is debasing to remain in office."

She would not join hands with the "assassins," as she called the insurrectionary forces. When Danton made overtures to her, she held coldly aloof. Her rejection of an alliance with this leader of the people has been termed a "folly," and she has been severely criticised therefor. She explained it as the result of an uncontrollable aversion, a physical repugnance. Danton, with his passionate face and voice and gestures, haranguing a street mob, was an avenging spirit in every way so different from the ideal she had imagined that she turned from him and his measures in loathing. He cured her of her love of revolution. He made a conservative of her.

It was at this period, when hopes, ambitions, dreams were falling from her and she was feeling bereft and desolate, that Madame Roland experi-

enced the deepest and most passionate love of
her life. Buzot, whom she had known in those
early days of the Revolution, between whom and
herself from the first there had existed an affinity, a "birth bond," one might almost say, of
thought and sentiment and daring courage, this
Buzot was in Paris. Thither he had come as
deputy to the convention, the new legislative
body that had been summoned to decide on the
future government of France.

Reflective, serious, earnest, Buzot satisfied
Madame Roland's most solemn needs. Moreover,
his elegant appearance, his courtly manners, his
deference, and his attentions charmed her. Then,
too, he was young, several years younger than
herself. He had not yet become contaminated by
contact with the world. He was not too practical
nor too experienced, nor cynical, nor pessimistic.
He still retained the illusions, the disinterestedness,
the purity, the confidence of youth. Madame
Roland could give her noblest to him, sure of a
response.

A long correspondence had drawn Buzot and
Madame Roland nearer and nearer together, had
intensified the sympathy that existed between them.
Thrown suddenly into constant intercourse with
each other, at a moment of grave crisis, their
common cause, their common danger, their close
affinity, united them in a love as unpremeditated as
it was inevitable.

MADAME ROLAND AT THE GUILLOTINE.
From a painting by Royer.

One of Madame Roland's friends once said of her that she possessed the "coquetry of virtue." She was forever reminding one of her duty, her constancy, and her devotion. Thus she had provoked Bosc and Lanthenas and Bancal, all her admirers since her marriage, and had kept matters between herself and them safe and "interesting."

Buzot was not the first man who, thus provoked, had loved Madame Roland. But he was the first man who had won Madame Roland's love. To the honor of Madame Roland it should be declared that she did not permit the love between Buzot and herself to shake her loyalty to Roland. When the Revolution was loosening all bonds, that of matrimony with the rest, and proclaiming man's right to happiness superior to any law, Madame Roland preserved, unimpaired, her fidelity to her marriage vows and her belief in the sanctity of the home.

However, with her "sentimental need of frankness," she could not forbear forcing upon Roland a confession of her love. The old man received the news stoically. But his heart was broken. The situation became tense and painful. Madame Roland thus described it: "My husband, excessively sensitive on account of his affection and his self respect, could not endure the idea of the least change in his empire; he grew suspicious, his jealousy irritated me. He adored me, I sacrificed myself for him, and we were unhappy."

Yet, in the midst of this so distressing state of affairs, the public cause was not neglected. It was attended to with unabated interest and fervor. Roland ran his Bureau of Public Opinion, scattering so far as he was able the vague teachings of the Girondist school. Madame Roland aided him, as previously, in all his literary labors and interviewed people for him. And Buzot, from his seat in the convention, defended the characters of Madame Roland and her husband and fought the " Mountain " bitterly and fiercely. No one in all the convention was more sensitive, more idealist, more indifferent to public applause than he. He was uncompromising, passionate in his denunciation of the Reign of Terror. His attitude was Madame Roland's attitude. The three worked together unselfishly and nobly. They gave no sign of their own inward struggles. To all appearances they had no desires, no aims, other than the country's welfare.

Theirs was the energy of despair. They knew that they were laboring for a lost cause. Daily the position of the Girondists became more untenable. Ever since the September massacres, when they had taken a stand against the insurrectionary movement, libels had been posted against them, the public journals published all manner of scandals concerning them. In these journals Madame Roland figured conspicuously. She was represented as having France " in leading strings," and was accused of being the real Minister of the

Interior, of squandering the national funds, and pulling down Marat's posters.

In December she was summoned before the bar of the Convention to answer to the charge of treason brought against her husband. Her appearance and her pertinent replies were loudly applauded, and she was awarded the honors of the session. For Madame Roland, this was an opportunity, a chance to display her powers. Heretofore she had been only an actor behind the scenes. Now she stepped upon the stage and spoke directly to her audience. One saw in her bearing a radiant enjoyment of this active part.

The time was not far distant when she would take her place among the prominent actors; the days of her imprisonment were close at hand. Dangers were increasing; soon to insult and libel attacks upon her personal safety were added. The Hotel of the Interior was raided repeatedly by a threatening mob. "It seemed," wrote a friend who was upon the scene, "that every night would be the last of her life." Flight was counselled, but Madame Roland, desirous of setting an example of firmness to the world, remained at her post until her husband's resignation in January.

Her fall and her husband's were simultaneous with that of their friends, the Girondists. On May 31 a deputation presented itself at the Rolands' apartment in the Rue de la Harpe with an order for the arrest of the ex-minister. Roland, however, succeeded in eluding the officials and making his escape. Madame hastened to the Convention, hoping by means of her beauty, her intelligence, and her eloquence to obtain a hearing and secure her husband's release and pardon. She found all entrances barred. The Assembly was in an uproar which, she learned later, meant a demand for the arrest of the Girondist leaders, Brissot, Vergniaud, Gaudet, Gensenné, and those others known as the "twenty-two." Madame Roland had to retire with her purpose unfulfilled.

In the early morning of the next day came her own arrest. She offered no resistance to her captors. She was proud to be persecuted, she said, when talent and honor were being proscribed. She was glad, too, to be put in a position to decry publicly the tyranny of her enemies. To one who expressed surprise at sight of her weeping household, remarking, "These people love you," she replied: "I never have any one about me who does not."

With an air of quiet dignity and a firm, intrepid step, she proceeded to the Abbayé. The savage cries of "à la Guillotine" that met her on the street, the brutality of guards and jailers which she noted upon her arrival at the prison, the sound of the tocsin ringing all night, the foul smells, the oaths and obscenity by which she was surrounded, could not shake her profound calm. She was lifted by sentiment and enthusiasm above material considerations.

From her captivity at the Abbayé Madame Roland was set free on June 25, only to be rearrested immediately and confined in the prison of Sainte Pélagie. There she remained until her removal to the Conciergerie, two weeks before her death, November 8. For one of less exalted spirit and less energetic mind, these long months of imprisonment must have passed without purpose and without resource. With Madame Roland it was otherwise. She drew inspiration from them. For her they were the moment of her trial. She had entered upon the stage of public virtues, she believed. She felt the eyes of all posterity upon her. The time had come, she thought, for her to range herself with the spirits of antiquity. She must act nobly, endure bravely, in order to be enrolled among those chosen ones. "With Socrates" she must "drink the hemlock;" "with Agis" she must "bend her neck to the axe."

These inward convictions were Madame Roland's one stimulus, her sole comfort. Of outward helps she had none. She was separated from her child. Her husband was in hiding. Buzot, whom she loved, had been proscribed by the "Mountain" on June 2, and was a fugitive. Her friends, the majority of them, were imprisoned, threatened with the penalty of death. As to her own fate she was under no illusion. Clearly she saw before her the awful shadow of the guillotine. All her early hopes and dreams and happiness were "sunk in

blood and mire." Her "beautiful Plutarchian republic " had vanished, dispelled by " the horror and
corruption of one city." Only from the inexhaust-
ive springs of her own soul did she derive her heroic strength and courage.

Viewed in her most lofty attitude, the pedestaled
position which she had assumed, Madame Roland
seems to us cold, remote, and unreal. It is, perhaps, pleasanter to view her in her more human as-
pects. Her triumphant cheerfulness and industry,
which did not fail her even at her prison door, fills
us with admiration. She was lodged in a rude and
stuffy little cell. So revolting were the people
by whom she was surrounded that she rarely left
her "cage." From the street, beneath the grating of her window, she could hear the hawkers of
Père Duchesne's journal shouting her name, coup-
ling it with calumnies which the market people
caught up, declaring against her loudly and rudely.
She endeavored to shut all this from her consciousness. With flowers which the faithful Bosc sup-
plied, and with books which her friends lent her,
she transformed her cell into an abode so pleasant
that her jailers called it "Flora's Pavilion." Here
she led a busy life. In the morning she sketched
and studied English, the essay of Shaftsbury on
virtue and Thompson's poetry. After dinner her
serious work began.

This serious work was her writing. To vindicate
her friends, her husband, and herself in the eyes of

posterity, to secure in history the recognition that her own generation had denied, this was her purpose. Historical notes, private memoirs, last thoughts fell rapidly from her pen. All was done easily, gracefully, and with a real joy in the telling. Critics have seen fit to ridicule the spirit of self-adulation which characterizes these productions. But when one takes into consideration the author's aim and the stress under which she wrote, one finds this spirit less humorous than pathetic. We see the poor prisoner in her cell, misjudged and calumniated, robbed of all she held most dear, her family, her friends, and the cause which she had so fondly and so ardently cherished, we behold her traversing alone the solemn Valley of the Shadow. Her consciousness of her own rectitude consoles her. We would be unkind, indeed, could we not forgive her this consolation.

She wrote of her mother and her father, of fair Mendon, of the Convent of the Congregation, of Sophie, of her quiet, studious, happy youth. As she told her story, the prison receded and with it her many sorrows and the thought of her approaching death. The old days returned. She lived her youth again, loving it, idealizing it.

She was interrupted, however. At different times news was brought her of some fresh atrocity of the Convention, of the arrest of one friend, of the condemnation and death of another; of the trial of the Girondists to which, she said, she had

waited to be called, "as a soul in pain awaits its
liberator," but to which she was not called; of the
execution of the twenty-one; Buzot was being
tracked from hiding-place to hiding-place, she
was informed, his discovery was almost certain;
Bosc, whom up to the middle of October she had
seen regularly, was proscribed and obliged to fly;
she could no longer receive direct news of her child
and her husband.

Her sadness and her despair became intense. In
many places tears stained her manuscript. Her
narrative stopped suddenly here and there " as
with a cry or sob." Her self-control, her pride,
her courage were almost more than human, but
there were times when her anguish was mightier
than these. " Before you she collects her strength,"
said an attendant to her fellow captives, " but in
her own cell she remains, sometimes for hours,
leaning against her window weeping." " Alas ! "
wrote Madame Roland in one of her last letters to
Bosc, " I know now what it is, the malady that the
English call heartbreak."

As the hour of her death approached, no one
could have had greater proof than Madame Roland
that she was beloved. The friend of her girlhood,
Henriette Cannet, the gay, the impulsive, the kind-
hearted, since married, a widow and childless,
visited her in her prison, offering to change gar-
ments with her, to take her place and risk death
for her. Madame Roland refused this proffer of

help as she did all others that would endanger another. To Buzot and Roland, both of whom were eager to attempt her escape, she wrote entreating them to make no imprudent efforts on her behalf. "It is by saving your country that you deliver me," she declared. She urged them, so long as they breathed and were free, to think only of their country, to live only for their country. "Brutus on the field of Philippi despaired too soon," she said.

Dying before her lover and her husband, Madame Roland was spared the knowledge of their failures and tragic deaths. Of Buzot it is related that when news reached him of her death, he said nothing, but was for several days like one "who has lost his senses." He was a hopeless fugitive at the time. After days of wandering, privation, and despair, the end came to him, no one knows just how. His body, beside that of Petion, was found in a wheat field, half eaten by wolves. As for Roland, he received the word that his wife had been guillotined as his own death warrant. He made a will providing for Eudora, said good-bye to the friends who were sheltering him, and proceeded to a retired spot on the roadside beneath the shade of a tree. There he seated himself and deliberately ran a cane sword into his breast. The next morning he was discovered dead, with this note on his person, "I left my refuge as soon as I heard that my wife had been murdered. I desire to remain no longer in a world covered with crime."

Madame Roland's death had more of glory in it
than those of her lover and husband. On November 1 she was confined in the Conciergerie, the
prison above the door of which was written the warning to abandon hope. The day before the Girondists had left it to go to their execution. The
inmates of the prison were just recovering from
the shock of that last horror. They looked with
curiosity, mingled with pity, upon the illustrious
woman who was entering, the friend of the men
who had just departed, whose own fate they knew
and knew that she herself knew was a foregone conclusion. They could discover no sign of weakness in
her bearing. Never had she been calmer, more
assured than at this moment when she was warned
that she must abandon hope.

The glimpses that we have of her from the pens
of her fellow-prisoners bring her before us very
attractively. " From the time of her arrival,"
wrote one, " the apartment of Madame Roland
became an asylum of peace in the bosom of this
hell. If she descended into the court, her simple
presence restored good order, and the abandoned
women there, on whom no other power exerted an
influence, were restrained by the fear of displeasing
her. She gave alms to the most needy, and to all
counsel, consolation, and hope." And another
said, " Something more than is generally found in
the look of woman beamed from her eyes, which
were large, dark, and brilliant. She often spoke

to me at the grating with the freedom and energy
of a great man. We used to gather round her and
listen in a kind of admiring wonder."

On the day after her arrival she was questioned
by the Tribunal. Two days later she was further
examined. She went from the prison, composed.
She returned deeply agitated, her eyes wet with
tears. All that she could say, she discovered, was
useless. She was the friend of the Girond.
Therein was her great crime.

On November 7 the witnesses against her were
heard. The Girondists had frequented Madame
Roland's house. That was the substance of the
testimony. Nothing further could be proved
by it.

The night of that day Chauveau Lagarde, a
courageous young lawyer, who was ambitious to
undertake Madame Roland's defence, called upon
her. She listened to what he had to say attentively, but without hope. When he had finished,
she did not speak, but drew a ring from her finger
and handed it to him. The young man understood
the act to be one of farewell. " Madame," he said,
much affected, " we shall meet to-morrow after the
sentence." " To-morrow," she replied, " I shall
not be alive. I value your services, but they
might prove fatal to you. You would ruin yourself without saving me. Spare me the pain of
putting the life of a good man in danger. Do not
come to the court, for I shall disclaim you if you

do, but accept the only token my gratitude can offer.   To-morrow I shall exist no more."

The next day, November 8, was the trial.   That morning, as she left her cell to await her summons to the bar, it was noted that she had dressed herself with the utmost care.   She had never looked so radiant.   She wore a gown of white muslin trimmed with blonde lace and fastened with a black velvet girdle.   Her dark hair flowed loosely below her waist.   Comte Bengnot joined her.   " Her face," he wrote, " seemed to me more animated than usual, and there was a smile on the lips.   With one hand she held up the train of her robe ; the other she abandoned to the prisoners who pressed forward to kiss it.   Those who realized the fate that awaited her sobbed about her and commended her to God.   Madame responded to all with affectionate kindness.   She did not promise to return, she did not say she was going to her death, but her last words to them were touching counsels.   .   .   . I delivered my message to her in the passage.   She replied in a few words spoken in a firm voice.   She had begun a sentence when two officers from the interior called her to the bar.   At this summons, terrible for another, she stopped, pressed my hand, and said, ' Good-bye, sir, it is time.'   Raising her eyes, she saw that I was trying to repress my tears. She seemed moved and added but two words, ' Have courage.' "

The tribunal awaited her and the charge of being

an accomplice in a "horrible conspiracy against the unity and indivisibility of the republic, the liberty and surety of the French people."

She came from her trial with the look as of one acquitted. But to the inquiring glances of her friends, she answered with a gesture that signified death. The cart in which she was to make her last journey stood ready in the court-yard.

Many before her had taken that jolting journey from the Conciergerie to the Place de la Guillotine. No one had travelled it with "a more sublime indifference to its terrors" than she. One who saw her as she passed described her as standing upright and calm in the tumbrel, her eyes shining, her color fresh and brilliant, with a smile on her lips, as she tried to cheer her companion, an old man overcome by the fear of approaching death. The mob followed and cursed her, but they could not reach the heights where her soul had soared.

At the foot of the scaffold she paused, asking for pen and paper to write "the strange thoughts that were arising in her." Her request was refused. Sanson, the executioner, grasped her arm and urged her to mount. She drew back, begging that her companion, the old man, be permitted to go first and thereby escape the pain of seeing her die. Sanson objected. It was the rule, he said, that the woman must die first. She looked into his face, smiling. "Can you refuse a lady's last request?" she asked. Sanson complied.

At length her turn came.   White robed and with
flowing hair, the smile still lingering on her lips,
and "the look as of a great man" shining in her
eyes, she ascended the scaffold.   As they were
binding her to the plank, her gaze rested on the
statue of liberty erected to celebrate the tenth of
August.   "O, liberté," she exclaimed, "comme on
t' a jouée."   Her number was called.   Her life was
told.

Perhaps no scene in the whole drama of Madame
Roland's life is more fitting than this closing one.
The thoughts which she had been forbidden to
express, we may be sure, were thoughts of elation,
even of joy.   She was dying the death of which
she had dreamed — the death of the warrior, young,
brave, and defiant, of one slain honorably in the
fight.   With her prophetic vision, she looked into
the future, saw the end of the evil days, saw order
and peace restored to her land, and saw her own
name, as the name of a hero, inscribed in her
country's story.   And, in her heart, forever constant in its fervor, she thanked God that she had
been permitted to make this sacrifice.

MADAME LE BRUN.

Born at Paris, April 16, 1755.
Died at Paris, May 29, 1842.

" The gentle painter of portraits who was everybody's friend."
— *Tallentyre*.

WE all know Madame Le Brun. We have seen her with her palette and her canvass; and again in the straw hat that suggests the famous painting by Rubens; and yet again with her daughter in her arms and the light of sweet maternity shining in her eyes. She appears before us in a variety of poses, yet she is always the same — curly haired, simply dressed, and with that suggestion of a smile parting her lips and softly lighting her pretty, oval face. We are, of course, attracted to her. We are interested to learn her story.

She herself has told her story in her memoirs. She has told it naïvely, vivaciously, and in a way that constantly reminds us of that smile which we behold in all her portraits of herself.

Her life was not exciting or eventful. She was not one to go down to the depths. She lived, for the most part, peaceably, pleasantly, graciously, on the surface. She was an artist and a Bohemian, careless of money, regardless of the future, yet kind and generous and friendly to all. She was irresponsible, a little eccentric perhaps, yet everybody loved her.

When Madame Le Brun was making the journey to Naples, her travelling companion was a gentleman of unenthusiastic temperament. As they were crossing the Pontine marshes together, madame called his attention to a shepherd seated on the banks of the canal, his sheep browsing in a field carpeted with flowers, and beyond the sea and Cape Circée. " This would make a charming picture," she said. " The sheep are all dirty," the gentleman replied. Further on she expressed admiration for the clouds surrounding the line of the Appennines and lighted by the setting sun. " Those clouds," he said," only promise us rain for to-morrow." And later, when the city was in sight, and they were passing between hedges of wild rose and scented myrtle, she could not repress an exclamation of delight. Her companion shrugged his shoulders. " I prefer the sunny slopes of Bordeaux that promise good wine," he observed.

Madame Le Brun, we may be sure, was not sorry to say good-bye to this uncongenial gentleman. She called him her " extinguisher." Fortunately she did not encounter many " extinguishers " in her life. Everywhere she met with sympathy, appreciation, and success.

Upon her entry into Naples, and always, the world was a picture for Madame Le Brun. And it is as a picture that her book of memoirs reflects

MADAME LÉ BRUN.
From the painting by herself.

the world. This book has no chronology or sequence; it discloses no theories or systems. But it is full of light and color and anecdote and amusing comment.

Reading the memoirs of Madame Le Brun, making with her the tour of the continent, we, too, behold the world with artist's eyes. At Venice we float down the Grand Canal in a gilded gondola, and see the Doge draw the ring from his finger and throw it into the waves, and we hear a thousand guns from the shore announcing this marriage of the Doge to the sea. At Naples we sit in Sir William Hamilton's casino and watch the small boys dive for pennies in the blue waters of the bay. At St. Petersburg we behold the breaking up of the ice on the Neva. We follow the progress of those daring spirits who cross the river, jumping from block to block of floating ice, and of that triumphant one who, having been the first to reach the further shore in a boat, presents the emperor with a silver cup, and receives it back filled with gold from the imperial hand. In the presence of scenes so picturesque and brilliant, dull things, such as dates and facts, which things, indeed, appear to have had no existence for Madame Le Brun, are quite forgotten. With her it is enough to drift along with eyes alert and a heart in tune with nature and humanity.

It is thus she herself drifted into the world. Elizabeth Louise Vigée she was called. At first she was remarkable only because of her talent. With her deep-set eyes and her pale, thin face she was not at all pretty. Her mother, who was beautiful and proud, preferred Elizabeth's younger brother, a handsome, precocious little fellow. But Elizabeth was her father's favorite. Monsieur Vigée, a kindly Bohemian sort of man, was himself an artist of moderate ability. He was delighted when one evening his little daughter, then seven years of age, brought him a picture of a man with a beard which she had drawn by lamplight. " Thou wilt be a painter, my child," he said, " if ever there was one."

Elizabeth drew always and everywhere, during study hours and play hours, on her copy books, on the wall, and on the sand. She was placed in a convent at the age of six, and remained there until she was eleven. When she was twelve years old her father died. The family was poor, and mademoiselle's talent was soon turned to account. The painters Doyen and Briard instructed and encouraged her. She painted portraits and landscapes and sold them. The money that they brought in not only supported herself, but helped to pay her mother's housekeeping expenses and bought her brother's school-books for him.

She worked earnestly and industriously. She haunted the Louvre and the Palace of the Luxembourg, and copied paintings by Rubens and Rembrandt and Vandyke and several heads of young

girls by Greuze. She made the acquaintance of
the painter Joseph Vernet. He gave her excellent
advice. "My child," he said, "do not follow any
particular school. Nature is the best master. If
you study it diligently you will never get into any
mannerisms."

Meanwhile, mademoiselle, who was absorbed in
her work and had no time to dream of beaux and
parties, had nevertheless grown pretty. Even her
beautiful mamma, who had always been so critical,
was satisfied with the appearance of her daughter.
Certain young men who came to her studio to have
their portraits painted by her were something more
than satisfied. They wanted to gaze at her with
tender glances (*las yeux tendres*). But she, the
little tease, always painted them with "eyes
averted," and at the least wandering of those eyes
in her direction arrested them with a demure, "I
am just at the eyes, monsieur."

It was not long before Elizabeth's beautiful
mamma presented her with a step-father. She did
not like her *beau pere*. She called him detestable.
The money that her painting brought in he appropriated. She, who was always so generous and free
with her money, forgave this. But she could not
forgive his wearing the clothes that had once
belonged to her own dear papa.

It was as much as anything to escape from this
beau pere that Mademoiselle Vigée consented to
marry Monsieur Le Brun. Monsieur Le Brun was

the owner of some valuable masterpieces of art.
He lent them to Mademoiselle Vigée to copy. He
became interested in mademoiselle's talent. There
was a fortune in it he thought. He determined to
marry it.

Mademoiselle Vigée was twenty years old when
she became the wife of Monsieur Le Brun. That
freshness, that delicacy, that sweetness which she
put into her pictures was in her own young soul.
She had lived all her life in her painting, her one
passion. She had read and studied very little.
She was as innocent as a child. On the day of her
wedding, on her way to church, she kept asking
herself, "Shall I say 'yes' or shall I say 'no'?"
It was a toss-up whether or not she should marry
Monsieur Le Brun, and just by chance the "yes"
had it.

She found she had exchanged old troubles for
new ones. Her husband was as prodigal with the
money she made as her *beau pere* had been. He
dissipated it completely, and she was able to save
only a few francs for herself.

For a while, to increase her income, she took
pupils. One morning she entered her studio to
find that her pupils had constructed a swing there
and were having a jolly time with it. She delivered them a little lecture on their levity. But the
swing proved too enticing for their mistress, who
was as young and blithe and girlish as any of her
pupils. She suddenly broke off her lecture,

laughed, and tried the swing herself. This episode decided her that she was too lively to be a teacher. She dismissed her class, and told them not to come again.

In truth she had no time for teaching. She had too many portraits on her hands. She could not execute all her orders. Court ladies, noblemen, men of mark, Calonne, minister of Finance, the queen herself, none were too great to sit before this charming girl artist with the clever brush. They all praised her work and courted her and loved her.

She made many friends, and was being asked out constantly. At first, having a strong liking for good company and merriment, she accepted all her invitations. One day, however, when she was dressed to go out and waiting for her carriage, she went to her studio for a moment, just to look at one of her portraits she said. Before she knew what she was doing, she was sitting down opposite her easel and working busily. When she came to get up she found she had been sitting on her palette. The condition of her gown, all smeared with paint, convinced her that she could not combine work and frivolity. She determined thereafter to devote all of the precious daylight to her art, and to make only evening engagements.

She was a careless, irresponsible young woman, this charming artist. Her friends sometimes called her a "tomboy." In her blouse and with

her round curly head she looked, when at work,
very like a mischievous little boy. She made no
preparations for the reception of her daughter in
the world. On the day that the child was born
she spent all her time before her easel painting her
" Venus tying the wings of Cupid." She was so
lost in her art that she had no other thought, until
Madame Verdun, an old friend, came and reminded
her.

It was different when she had her little daughter in her arms. Then she experienced a happiness
greater even than that which her art had given her.
She could now paint the better for her love she said.

It was in 1779, shortly after the birth of her
daughter, that Madame Le Brun painted her first
portrait of the queen. After that she painted
numerous portraits of Her Majesty. At first
Madame Le Brun felt shy in the presence of the
queen. One day, in embarrassment, she dropped her
brushes. Marie Antoinette herself stooped and
picked them up, and with a kind, encouraging smile
put the modest little artist at her ease. After that
they were very good friends, and sang duets together during the sittings. To herself, however,
Madame Le Brun was forced to confess that the
queen did not always sing " in tune."

Madame also painted the portrait of monsieur,
brother of the king, afterwards Louis XVIII.
He, too, sang in her presence, songs that seemed to
her decidedly " rubbish." His voice was still less

in tune than the queen's, madame decided. "How do you think I sing, Madame Le Brun?" he inquired. "Like a prince," she replied. Shy and unconventional though she was, she was still a little of a diplomat.

While she was painting these portraits of the royal family, Madame Le Brun made the acquaintance of the king. He talked with her, and at his praise she, who was always so naïve and charming, blushed with pleasure. "I do not understand much about painting," he said, "but you have made me love it."

This patronage of "the elite" helped to establish Madame Le Brun's success. She was already recognized as a celebrity. She was applauded at the theatre and at the Académie Francaise. She was made a member of the Royal Academy of Painting.

All this time she lived very modestly in the Rue de Clery. Most of the house was occupied by Monsieur Le Brun's fine collection of pictures. Only a very small suite of rooms was reserved for the mistress. But here she resided contently, and worked busily and received her friends. Ladies and gentlemen of the court and men of mark in literature and art attended her receptions. She *said* that they came to see each other, but they themselves knew, if she did not, that they came to see her. She was delightfully natural and unceremonious with her guests. When there were not chairs enough to go round some sat on the floor. Occasionally the fattest of them, the Marshal de Noailles, had difficulty in getting up again. Then every one laughed. Madame entertained her company with music and impromptu theatricals, and once she gave them a Greek supper. She dressed them all in antique costumes borrowed from her studio. They ate to the accompaniment of a chorus of Glück's and the music of the lyre, and were served by madame's daughter and another little girl, two pretty children, each bearing an ancient vase. The whole affair was very novel and picturesque. Madame's artistic touch was evident in all she did, the social as well as the professional.

It was at this time, in the midst of Greek suppers, applause, theatres, operas, and infinite portrait painting, that Madame Le Brun went to Louveciennes. There could not have been brought together two more contrasting women than madame the artist and madame the courtesan, — the one of unaffected prettiness and artless grace, knowing little of the world but its art, innocent and sweet and flowerlike, a girl still; the other a notorious beauty, well versed in all the wickedness of the world, coquettish and full of wiles, in spite of her forty-five years, her wrinkles, and her approaching stoutness.

Madame Le Brun painted Madame du Barry in various poses, and she walked with her in her beautiful pavilion and sat with her in her beautiful salon before the fire and listened to her talk of

MADAME LE BRUN AND HER DAUGHTER.
From the painting by herself.

Louis XV. and his court. It was an age when the innocent mingled freely with the guilty. This intercourse, however, did not harm Madame Le Brun. She worked industriously, and smiled to herself in an amused, satiric sort of way at du Barry's confidences. And when she left Louveciennes, she carried with her a good and blithe and bonny heart unchanged.

Madame's visit to Louveciennes was paid on the eve of the Revolution. When that horror dawned, and she saw a landscape bereft of all beauty, hideous and stained with blood, her artist's soul was shaken. She shut her eyes and ran away. Of course it was not brave of her to do this, but then Madame Le Brun was never noticeably brave. She was not a warrior or a hero or anything noble and imposing. She was just an artist and a very womanly woman. Therefore her rapid exit was quite in character.

She did not stop running or open her eyes, so to speak, until she was in Italy. There the sky, the sunshine, the mountains, and the treasures of art which she visited restored beauty to her sight and brought comfort to her soul. Later the shores of the blue Danube and the midnight twilight of the Neva attracted her. We find her at Sienna seated in the doorway of an inn, contemplating a view of garden and canal, listening to a concert of birds and water-fall and rustling trees, forgetting, meanwhile, her supper, until the servant of the inn comes to remind her of it. And at Bologna we behold her traversing the galleries and commenting on the pictures, until the guide stands mute before her and turns to inquire of the bystanders, "Who is this lady? I have led many great princesses through this gallery, but never any one so well informed as she." And again we see her taking solitary walks in the environs of Rome, admiring the grandeur of the Appennines and the rainbow colors in the sky. Often she has with her her daughter, whose childish prattle delights her. When the trees are still, the little voice whispers, "Look, mother, they seem to ask us to be silent." And when the wind agitates them, the girl clings, trembling, to the mother's skirts. "They are alive," she exclaims. "I tell thee they are alive." Finally we follow Madame Le Brun to England. There the dulness of English country life falls like a chill on her gay French spirits. She fidgets in the drawing-room that is full of ladies all embroidering in silence and of gentlemen all reading in silence. She proposes a moonlight walk, to which objection is straightway raised. She investigates the library and the picture-gallery. An exclamation of delight, which unconsciously escapes her, draws upon her looks of reproving surprise. She sighs. This atmosphere of studious calm is not her natural element.

Madame Le Brun was kept busy during her long sojourn. She painted many portraits. And she

had need of all this portrait painting. She had
come away with only a few francs, having left all
her money behind her in France for the maintenance of her extravagant husband. Unpractical
and childishly unmercenary, she took little thought
for her material welfare. It did not trouble her
that she was without fortune so long as she reserved
always her talent that could amass one.

She did care for comfort, however. Disagreeable
noises and smells distressed her very much. Yet,
wherever she travelled, an annoying fate was forever thrusting them in her way. Now a dancing
master instructed his classes over her head ; or a
band practised its music there ; or the town pump
was just outside her window, and began its work at a
provokingly early hour. Her neighbors had a habit
of cooking unsavory dishes. Sleep left her, and
her nose was offended repeatedly . The climax was
reached in London in a house in Portman square.
There she was waked at daybreak by piercing cries,
which, upon rising and popping her head out the
window, she traced to an enormous bird of East
Indian character caged in a window near by. That
same day she found in her cellar the graves of two
slaves. " What with corpses and birds," she protested, " it was really too much. I left the house
in Portman square."

Madame Le Brun travelled from court to court,
from academy to academy, from Paris to Rome, and
Rome to St. Petersburg. Meanwhile the Revolu-

tion advanced. She would not read the newspapers; she would not let any one talk to her of
her unhappy land. Yet she thought often of the
queen who had been kind to her and the king
who had praised her art, both of whom she loved
and lamented. Through all their vicissitudes, her
loyalty to the Bourbons never faltered. To the
day of her death she remained faithful to the old
régime and the ancient nobility.

She settled in St. Petersburg, having with her
always her daughter and her art, a twofold happiness. She was to lose a half of that happiness.
Her daughter, grown into a very pretty young
woman, much petted, much indulged, took a fancy
to a certain Monsieur Nigris, a man without talent,
fortune, or family, whose soft ways and melancholy glances were his only recommendation.
Mademoiselle cried for him, as in her childhood she
had cried for some pretty toy, and Madame Le
Brun, who could deny her nothing, consented to
the marriage of mademoiselle with this gentleman
of her choice. It was madame's good-bye to her
daughter. After the wedding she seldom saw her
little girl, and when she did see her, the child's
taste for bad company distressed the mother's heart.
An exchange of visits brought more pain than joy.
Later, when her daughter died, Madame Le Brun's
grief was very great. At sight of the dear, lovely,
altered face she fainted. All the naughtinesses of
the poor little thing were blotted out of her mem-

ory, she said, and she saw her as in the days of her childhood.

Her daughter married, her canvas crowded with all the sovereigns of Europe, and all the heads crowned by genius, and the Revolution at an end, Madame Le Brun returned to Paris. She arrived during the consulate. She met with a warm welcome. Her husband had decorated the house handsomely to receive her. The trouble had been his. Therefore she was pleased and grateful. That the cost would certainly be hers did not annoy her greatly. At her first appearance in public, at a concert, the audience turned and applauded her. She was much touched, and answered with tears. Her old friends, those who remained, called upon her. Greuze and Madame Bonaparte were among her visitors. It was pleasant to be again in France, which, though changed, was still France, social, polite, and light-hearted as of old. She was at home.

Madame Le Brun lived on, painting portraits, entertaining and visiting her friends, and finding in her niece, Eugénie Le Brun, a second daughter. To the end it was the beautiful she sought, the beautiful she found. And it is a bit of the beautiful that she has contributed to the world.

MADAME DE STAËL.

Born at Paris, April 22, 1766.
Died at Paris, July 24, 1817.

" A woman great and magnanimous even in the inmost
reaches of her soul."— *Schlegel*.

" I WISH that I could see you asleep," one of
Madame de Staël's friends once said to her. " I
should like to feel sure that you sometimes close
your eyes and stop thinking." It was impossible
to imagine her any way but wide-awake, overflowing with thought and energy and life.

Even to-day it is difficult to realize that those
dark, " magnificent " eyes have closed forever, that
the great de Staël is sleeping the eternal sleep.
We read of her and forget realities, as we fall
under the spell of her magnetic personality. She
seems still to be holding court at Coppet, talking
to an enchanted audience, wielding her sceptre, the
leafy bough that a servant placed every day
beside her plate. We listen and applaud and
render homage to the queen of conversation.

A rival once declared of Madame de Staël that
she was nothing more than a " talking machine."
It was a clever phrase, but it was undeserved. No
one was ever less a " machine " than Madame de

MADAME DE STAËL.
From the painting by Mlle. Godefroy.

Staël, who was eminently sensitive, generous, and fervid among women. Her mind was great, but her heart was greater, and her genius sprang equally from both.

Madame de Staël's genius evinced itself at an early age. She was an erratic, precocious, unduly thoughtful little maiden. Never pretty even in childhood, but with engaging ways and a remarkable originality and maturity of mind, she attracted the attention of her parents' friends. Seated on a low hassock at Madame Necker's feet, she may be truly said to have received with her mamma. Marmontel, Raynal, Grimm, the gravely ironical Abbé Morellet, all the famous personages who frequented the Necker salon, bent to speak to the strange, old-young child. A portion of the homage they had awarded unreservedly to the mother they now bestowed upon the daughter. They delighted to draw out the little Germaine, for so she was called, to see the light of a wonderful intelligence break in her eyes and to listen to her quick, pertinent, and wise replies.

For the mother who sat above her, like a queen upon her throne, receiving the compliments of her distinguished guests, the daughter entertained a profound awe. In that beautiful, pale, severely gracious presence she showed herself submissive and restrained. One seeing her only thus would never have suspected the ardent, impetuous, passionate nature that was really hers.

Madame Necker, who was the daughter of a
Swiss parson, and who had inherited the paternal
chastity and piety, was an eminently virtuous lady.
Moreover, before her marriage she had been a
school-mistress. Therefore the most rigorous of
moral precepts and a host of pedagogic theories
were brought to bear upon her little daughter.
Under her mother's tutelage, Germaine read and
prayed, studied and dissertated and conversed.
The result was that at the age of eleven, with her
amazing powers of intellect, she had developed
into a very erudite and accomplished, but a most
unchildlike, individual.

Meanwhile papa was in the background. He
was a very busy, very important man, the Minister
of Finance of France. He had very little time to
devote to his young daughter. He was more
indulgent than mamma, however. During those
infrequent moments when father and daughter
were together, Germaine did not stand in awe of
him. She dared to frisk before him, to play the
child, to show him how very lively and amusing
she could be. Necker seldom reprimanded her.
Instead he laughed at her, and petted and caressed
her.

Germaine, with her alert perception, was
quick to note the difference between her father's
and her mother's attitudes towards herself. She
was as quick to appreciate the meaning of this
difference. One day, when she had offended and

had been sternly reproved by her mamma therefor, she could not repress her tears. Some one of the many frequenters of the Necker salon drew near and sought to comfort her. "Never mind," he whispered consolingly, "one kiss from your papa will make it all right again." Germaine regarded her friend gravely through her tears and, with a world of wisdom in her look, she answered, "Ah, yes, monsieur, papa thinks of my present happiness, mamma of my future."

The contemplation of that goal of future happiness to which Madame Necker so persistently pointed must have wearied somewhat Germaine's mischief-loving spirit. Though she was for the most part a very reverential and obedient daughter, there were occasional faint flashes of self assertion, brief glimpses of a gaiety, a frankness, a naïveté as irrepressible as her life. Now it happened that a company of play actors, paper kings and queens, drew her attention from her studies. Mamma frowned. The kings and queens were removed from mamma's scrutiny, and the play continued to the end. Again it happened that a guest passing through the Necker garden on his way to the house, felt a light, stinging blow on his hand. Turning to resent the assault, he beheld the assaulter, the little daughter of the house, peering at him roguishly from behind a tree. "Mamma wishes me to learn to use my left hand," she explained. "You see I am trying to do so."

And again, most significant of all, it happened
that once at table in the temporary absence of her
mother, Germaine threw a napkin across the table
at her papa and then, flying round to his side,
smothered his reproaches with her kisses. More
than that, she drew the dignified Necker into a
dance with her, a dance which ended abruptly
at sound of madame's returning footsteps. When
that august lady entered, father and daughter
had resumed their places, and nothing could
have been more decorous than their behavior.

In these instances Germaine revealed herself.
In spite of all the pedantry with which her youth
was crammed, she was still at heart natural,
rudely yet beautifully natural. However, these
instances were exceptional. Most of the time
she showed her training. She was a product of
the salon. The tinsel of society was upon her
and the little vanities and artificialities of the
world were manifest in all her conduct.

With her prodigious learning and remarkable
savoir faire, she quite amazed little Mademoiselle
Hüber, her cousin, a child of her own age, who
came to live with her and to be her companion.
Germaine, unused to children, fell instantly in
love with the pretty, dainty, aerial little mademoiselle. We can imagine the eloquence of the
glances, the ardor of the embraces, with which
she greeted her new found friend and vowed
" eternally to cherish " her. Impetuously she

began plying her with questions, not after the manner of children, but in very conversational and grown-up fashion. What were her favorite studies? Did she know any foreign languages? Had she ever been to the theatre? And when to the latter question her cousin answered that she had, Germaine, to use her own expression, was "transported." They would go often together, she declared, and afterwards would write down all those portions of the play which had interested them most. Oh, they would have a royal time.

In the evening of that first day of their acquaintance, Mademoiselle Hüber went with Germaine into the salon. She was herself a bright, observant child. She noted with admiring awe Germaine's ease and grace with the distinguished guests. She saw that it was the cleverest men who talked with Germaine. "They asked what she was reading," Mademoiselle Hüber afterwards related, "recommended new books to her, and talked to her of what she knew, and of what she had yet to learn."

Thus even so soon, at this period of Mademoiselle Hüber's advent, Germaine Necker was giving proof of her extraordinary powers. Intimations of her future greatness showed in her conversation and in the animation of her "great black eyes." It also expressed itself in an intense sensibility. This sensibility was such that praise of her parents brought tears to her eyes. The presence of famous personages, heroes and heroines of her young fancy, set her heart to palpitating. Like Manon Phlipon, she was a disciple of Rousseau, passionate in her enthusiasm for talent and virtue, and in her compassion for all suffering humanity. She liked to read of the Werthers, the Julies and the Clarisse Harlowes of literature. She cared only for that which made her weep.

The truth was she was paying the penalty of her prematurely developed mind. The excessive training to which she had been subjected by her mother was beginning to tell on her health. Tronchin was called in. He prescribed absolute rest from study, fresh air, and exercise. Thus cruelly did he shatter Madame Necker's ambitions and projects ; for, such was the authority of the celebrated physician, that she did not venture to raise an objection. Straightway and without cavil, Germaine was transported to Saint Ouen.

At Saint Ouen, the beautiful country seat of the Neckers, wandering in its shady avenues, reclining in its peaceful groves, and acting with her beloved cousin, Mademoiselle Hüber, improvised tragedies upon the lawns, with nothing to do but enjoy herself, Germaine regained her health and innate gaiety of spirit. Those instances of laughing, frolicking nature which had always been so rare with her became more frequent. She ceased to be an

infant phenomenon and was instead a child.
Madame Necker found her very commonplace, and
turned coldly from her. But her changed condition delighted her papa. He sought her company
and in her sallies of wit and playful humors found
recreation.

Estranged from her mother and drawn nearer
and nearer to her father, Germaine reserved her
awe for the one and gave to the other a profound
and adoring love. It is pleasant to contemplate
in a brilliant life, such as that of Germaine Necker
was destined to be, a love so pure and abiding as
hers for her father. One sees in it a counterpart
of Madame de Sevigné's for her daughter. Like
the love of the witty marquise, it amounted to a
passion. It filled her life. She listened to Necker's
tales of his boyhood, pictured him young, ardent,
and ambitious, and lamented that fate had not
made them contemporaries and united her destiny
eternally with his.

When Germaine was fifteen years of age, Necker
published his " Compte Rendu " and consequently
fell from power. He retired to Saint Ouen and
there a host of sympathetic and admiring friends
visited him and his family. From now on until
the time of her marriage, a period of five years,
Germaine enjoyed uninterruptedly the companionship of her parents and lived with them, in spite
of their so-called " disgrace," a triumphant and
highly intellectual life.

Of course, with her natural propensity for emotion, she early conceived a romantic attachment for one of the many who came to her home, a very conspicuous personage, the Monsieur Guibert later distinguished by the love of Mademoiselle de Lespinasse. This gentleman, with his engaging ways, captivated her as he had captivated other less impressionable maidens and, what is perhaps more agreeable to contemplate, he entertained at least a passing fancy for Necker's brilliant daughter. He wrote a "portrait" of her, in which he described her as a priestess of Apollo with dark, luminous eyes and black, floating curls and features that marked her for a superior destiny.

This portrait of Mademoiselle Necker by Monsieur Guibert was one of many read in the Necker salon. To the many Mademoiselle Necker contributed her share. And these portraits, executed by her with a frank exaggeration which was not without its charm, were not the only products of her pen. At the time of Necker's fall from power, when she was only fifteen years of age it should be remembered, she wrote her father an anonymous letter. This letter showed a perfect understanding of his position. Its style betrayed her. Moreover, as she advanced in her teens, she wrote ambitious tragedies and novelettes. She quite shocked her somewhat Calvinistic mamma with a play called "Sophie," which had for its subject the struggles of a young girl against her love for her guardian, a married man.

Her writing was done out of sight of her teasing papa. Necker exceedingly disliked authorship in a woman. He sought to dissuade his daughter from the pursuit of letters. He nicknamed her Mademoiselle de Sainte Ecritoire. But all his badinage could not suppress her literary effusions. These were the natural exhalations of her soul.

As time went on, however, and Germaine's twentieth birthday approached, her authorship was temporarily abandoned and forgotten. The question of her marriage arose and engrossed, to the exclusion of all else, the attention of the Necker family.

Formerly, while she was still a child, simple and naïve in spite of pedantry, Germaine had given her consideration to this question of her marriage. She had observed the great respect in which Gibbon, the famous English historian, was held by her parents, the pleasure which his conversation afforded them. She herself, it must be confessed, found him very corpulent and ugly and not at all to her taste. However, she waived all personal considerations, and very seriously, and in a spirit of duty and infinite love, proposed to her father and mother that she would marry their much revered friend. "We would live with you, of course, and you could hear Monsieur Gibbon talk forever and ever." We can imagine her expressing herself thus quaintly and in all sincerity. Needless to say, the sacrifice was not demanded of her. With the sanction of Monsieur and Madame

Necker, Gibbon remained a bachelor, and Germaine was reserved for fate in another shape than that of the almost spherical English historian.

The large fortune of Mademoiselle Necker, even more than her brilliant mind it is to be feared, attracted many suitors. Conspicuous among them were Prince George Augustus of Mechlenburg, brother of the reigning duke, William Pitt of England, and the Baron de Staël Holstein. Of these the Prince was so impudent as to declare that he desired the lady only on account of her enormous dower. His proposals were therefore rejected by Monsieur and Madame Necker with a becoming promptitude. Madame Necker favored the claims of Pitt. Her discerning mind appreciated his character and ability and interpreted them, no doubt, as marks of future greatness. She praised him to Germaine, and was displeased when that young lady turned a deaf ear. It was not the Englishman, but the Swedish baron whom Germaine preferred.

The reason of her choice was to be found in her love for her father. She could not endure the thought of leaving France and him for any husband. De Staël's virtue in her eyes, therefore, was his French residence.

Finding favor in the young lady's sight, the baron was encouraged to press his suit ardently. He had much in his favor. He was a favorite at court, a liberal like Necker, and, also, like Necker, a Protestant. Moreover, he had recently been appointed Swedish ambassador at the Court of France and, in view of the marriage, it had been arranged with his king, Gustavus, that he was to remain in that capacity for an indefinitely long term of years. Necker received him graciously, madame, who remembered Pitt, a little coldly. At length, after due consideration and negotiation, he was accepted. The marriage settlement was drawn up and signed by the king and queen and numerous other important personages, and on the fourteenth of January, 1786, the wedding, a very imposing one, took place.

It was by no means a marriage of love. The groom was thirty-seven, and interested in obtaining a fine fortune. The bride was twenty, in love with her father, and desirous of remaining always in his neighborhood. On both sides there was a friendliness, but nothing of a deep or enduring character. Indeed, the affair was quite manifestly one of convenience.

On the last night that she spent under her father's roof, Germaine was very serious. She thought of the future. But more than that she thought of the past. It seemed to her that in that moment, "as in that of death," all her deeds returned to her. She was possessed with a sadness, a regret, a desire to make right, in so far as she was able, all her past errors and failings. And quite naturally, in that "moment" of self-judgment, it

was not to her father, between whom and herself
there had never been a coolness, but to her mother
that she addressed herself. She wrote a farewell
letter to Madame Necker, wistfully breathing a
hope that she might be missed, generously blaming
herself for all past dissensions, and warmly expressing the tenderness which she "felt for her mother,
and which at that moment was so deep," she said,
" as to convince her that it had always been the
same." Thus in a spirit of sweet humility, asking
pardon for her faults, with a backward glance of
love for all that she was leaving, Germaine went
out from her father's home.

A brilliant and eventful life awaited her. Immediately she was presented at court and attracted
much attention there. The ultra-conventional
criticised her. They said, with a smile of worldly
wisdom and superiority, that she was very "simple" and that her self-assurance was certainly
"amusing;" and when she tore her gown and
omitted the third courtesy, they viewed her with
glances of horror; in their eyes she could not have
committed a more grievous offence. The young
madame, herself, however, only laughed. She
could exist without the patronage of the ultra-conventional. All the thinking people of France were
gathering round her in an admiring circle. She was
content in their society and did not miss the others.

Shortly after Madame de Staël's marriage, her
father was recalled to power. She herself, as soon

as she heard the news, in a jubilant frame of mind, hastened to Saint Ouen. To her congratulations her father responded sadly. "It is too late," he said. Madame Necker, too, shook her head. To her, as to her husband, it seemed that the outlook of France and his part therein were hopeless. But Madame de Staël would not listen to their forebodings. She was inspired with youthful ardor and unbounded confidence in her father. "Every day," she declared, warmly, "he will do something good and prevent something bad."

As the daughter of a minister and the wife of an ambassador, Madame de Staël's position had now become one of influence. Many distinguished men met in her parlors. Her house, indeed, was a rallying point not only for men like her father, who were monarchical and desired a constitution on the English model, but also for the more liberal politicians, such men as La Fayette, de Montmorency, and Narbonne, the constitutional royalists, who in '91 formed themselves into a powerful party.

With these men and with the intelligent portion of Parisian society in general, Madame de Staël's talents, equally with her wealth and position, gave her distinction. While every one was discussing politics and idealizing about the glorious future of humanity, she discussed and idealized so wisely and eloquently that she was soon installed the presiding genius in all such conversations. Moreover, her first publication, her " Letters on Jean Jacques," were being read and creating a sensation. Grimm described them as " a charming work " and eulogized them and their youthful author.

Madame de Staël's " Letters on Jean Jacques " disclosed for the first time the remarkable reaches of her mind and soul. They revealed vistas of thought which in her later works appeared developed and matured. Reading these letters, one beholds their author wandering in Elysian fields, following reverentially in the footsteps of Rousseau, yet drawn now and then from the path of his choosing, by her own audacious fancy, into new and untried ways. The letters are a pæan of praise to him, her " literary parent." But through them there sounds, clear and strong, her own " motif." Now it peals forth with all the lightness and ardor and hopefulness of youth. At this period of her existence there was, as she herself phrased it, " something of the Scotch air in the music of her life." The motif was rippling in the treble key. As yet it only suggested and had not developed those sombre chords " intense and sorrowful " which made the music of her later life.

The time was at hand, however, when the fierce thunder of the Revolution was to drown the music of her life, when in anguish she was to reproach herself " even for thought, as something too independent of grief." The Scotch air died in her heart for the first time when fate aimed its blow at her father. She was present at that dinner at which Necker received his communication from the king ordering him to leave France immediately and to depart in secrecy. She witnessed his reading of the letter in silence and calm, and did not suspect its contents. Dinner at an end, she saw her father and mother take leave of the company and drive off in their carriage and supposed, as did every one else, that they were bound on a pleasure trip.

Her indignation and sorrow, when the truth became known to her, may be imagined. Straightway, accompanied by her husband, she hastened to overtake her parents, and came up with them at Brussels. Therefore she was able to make with them the triumphant return. Her father, in compliance with the demand of the populace, was recalled. The people who loved him, because to him they were indebted for the double representation of the Third Estate, had prepared for him a glorious reception. The way back to Paris was strewn with roses. A jubilant crowd met him at the gates of every town and substituted themselves for horses and postilions. Everywhere he was greeted with shouts of "Vive Necker! Vive Necker!" Madame de Staël, looking into the enthusiastic faces of the people, lived the proudest and happiest moment of her life. At no other time did the Scotch air sing itself so joyously in her heart.

A few months more and she was to see those same faces, which now expressed love, expressing instead hate. She was to hear the cries of "Vive Necker" changed to curses and false accusations. She was to learn how fleeting a thing is the favor of the multitude. Because Necker was sympathetic in too many directions, because he was sorry for a tottering king and queen, nobility and clergy, as well as for a down-trodden people, because he opposed certain popular measures and stood a little in the way of the popular ascendancy, he was disregarded and thrust aside. He tendered his resignation and it was received without protest or regret. In a spirit of Quixotic magnanimity, he deposited two millions of his own property in the royal treasury and silently took his leave. His escape to Switzerland was through a growling, snarling mob. He was hounded to the very gates of his country. It appeared that France had forgotten his many faithful services and chose to consider him a traitorous stranger.

Madame de Staël soon followed her father to his Swiss retreat. She knew now that he had spoken truly when he said, "It is too late." Her young, bright, hopeful illusion had vanished. She stood face to face with the tragedy of his failure and of her country's danger. We can picture her seated by her father's side or walking with him along the margin of the beautiful lake, seeking with consoling words to cheer him, yet oppressed all the while with a sadness like his own and apprehensions for their country's safety.

Having made this visit of condolence to her father, Madame de Staël returned to Paris. She regarded that city as an arena for a struggle in which her services might be needed. As of old, the constitutional royalists rallied in her salon. Conspicuous among them was Narbonne, young, brilliant, charming. Madame was his friend, warmly, devotedly his friend. Some whispered that she loved him too dearly. Yet so simple, so frank, so open, so devoid of all art and coquetry was madame's love for this gentleman that in its presence slander halted, uncertain and abashed, and posterity is left in doubt. Through the influence of Madame de Staël, Narbonne was appointed in December of '91 Minister of War. He did not hold the office long. In a few months he was dismissed by his king and sent to serve for a while in the war on the frontier.

As the Revolution advanced and the Reign of Terror drew near, while proscriptions were the order of the day, and on all sides royalists and constitutionalists were perishing or fleeing, Madame de Staël, safe in her character of ambassadress, remained at Paris, ever watchful, active, and courageous in the cause of friendship. When at length the Baron de Staël was recalled by his government and the Tuileries were invaded, Necker wrote urging his daughter to join him. But Madame de

Staël would not leave so long as it was possible
that by staying she might rescue a friend.

Now it was in the interests of Narbonne that she
lingered. The terrible tenth of August had passed
and other days equally terrible had succeeded.
Narbonne was among the proscribed. Knowing
this, Madame de Staël sought him through the
bloody city, found him in his place of hiding,
brought him to her house, and concealed him there.
When the police agents came demanding Monsieur
de Narbonne, Madame de Staël was ready for them.
She took advantage of their ignorance, demanding
of them if they realized that they were violating
their rights in invading the house of an ambassadress (she took pains not to tell them that her
husband had been recently recalled) and warned
them that unless they desisted, Sweden, which was
dangerously near, would descend upon France.
Having first frightened them, Madame de Staël
next proceeded to pleasantries. She was very
witty and charming. Before the police agents
knew what was happening, they were being bowed
gracefully out of the house. Four days later,
Madame de Staël procured a false passport and by
means of it Monsieur de Narbonne was enabled to
escape to England.

Again it was to save Lally Tollendal and Jancourt that she delayed. Jancourt, a former member of the Legislative Assembly, and Lally Tollendal
had been sent to the Abbayé, which was only too

aptly termed "the ante-chamber of death." To many their doom seemed certain. Not so, however, to Madame de Staël, the cheerful, the determined, the indefatigable. She hastily ran over in her mind the names of the members of the Commune who sat in judgment on her friends, and bethought her of one Manuel, a man of literary pretensions, who she believed might be susceptible to flattery. At the democratic hour of seven in the morning she made an appointment with him and called upon him at his house. She appealed first to his vanity, then to his humanity. She spoke of the terrible times, of the uncertainty of all lives. "Think," she said, "in six months you may no longer have power. Save Lally and Jancourt. Reserve for yourself a sweet and consoling recollection when you may be proscribed." Her eloquence conquered. The next day she received a letter from Manuel informing her that Condorcet had obtained the liberation of Lally, and that he himself had released Jancourt in answer to her entreaties.

At length, having done all that she could for her friends, Madame de Staël decided to leave France. True, even at this final moment, to her life-preserving character, she planned to take with her the Abbé de Montesquion in the disguise of a domestic. He was given the passport of one of her servants and was to meet her at an appointed rendezvous.

The rendezvous was never reached, however, and the scheme failed in most alarming fashion. Madame de Staël's carriage had proceeded only a short distance on its outward-bound journey when it was surrounded by an angry mob and stopped. Madame was accused of seeking to take away proscribed royalists and was ordered to proceed to the Hotel de Ville under the command of a gendarme. Her carriage was straightway turned about and led, long and wearily, at a foot pace, through the crowd, amid cries of "Death."

Up the steps of the Hotel de Ville, on which same steps only the day following the Princess de Lamballe perished, between a double row of pikes, Madame de Staël mounted. She was conducted into the presence of Robespierre and a host of passionate people all shouting "Vive la Nation." Before this audience she immediately proceeded, forcibly and eloquently as was her way, to plead her right to depart as an ambassadress.

She might have spoken to deaf ears, had it not been for the opportune appearance of Manuel. He gave his word to the people that he would be responsible for her until the Commune should decide her fate, and escorted her and her maid to his own house. There, in the same room in which she had entreated for Lally and Jancourt, she remained for six hours "dying," as she herself expressed it, "of hunger, thirst, and fear." In the evening Manuel, himself pale with horror at

the scenes which he had that day witnessed, came
to her. He told her that he had obtained a passport for herself and one maid; and that she was
to leave Paris the next morning under the escort
of a gendarme.

The next morning several suspected aristocrats
came to say good-bye to Madame de Staël. She did
not send them away. She received them warmly,
kissing them, even, we may imagine, under the
eyes of the gendarme, imploring him tremulously
meanwhile to be " discreet." Thus, mindful of
her friends to the very last and sick at heart,
Madame de Staël took her departure.

She went directly to Switzerland, to Coppet, to
her father and mother. There nature, beautiful
and vast, awaited her. But nature did not comfort
her. Rather it surprised and hurt her. She
mourned over the sorrows of her friends and her
mutilated country even in the presence of Mount
Blanc and Lake Leman. She reproached the
mountains for their undisturbed and lofty grandeur, the lake for its bright, careless calm. Her
soul cried then, as later her pen wrote : " Oh, earth !
steeped in tears and blood, thou bringest forth
thy fruits and flowers unceasingly ! Hast thou,
then, no pity for man and can his dust return into
thy maternal bosom without causing it to bound ? "

With the birds singing about her, she heard only
from afar the strokes of the guillotine and each
blow struck her heart. And with all of fair Swit-

zerland before her to attract her gaze, she looked
behind sadly, pitifully, at poor, disfigured France.
She loved the victims who were falling there. She
was in turn a sister, a brother, a wife, a daughter,
a son, a father, and most of all, she was a mother
— so tender, so protecting was her love for all that
suffering humanity.

Her efforts were directed toward giving such
relief as she was able. Coppet became an asylum
for proscribed emigrés. Thither came Mathieu
de Montmorency, Jancourt, the Princess de Poix,
and Madame de Simiane. Madame de Staël constantly was engaged devising plans that would
enable proscribed persons to escape from France.
She procured for them Swiss passports in which
they were given Swiss names. She sent her
agents to them, and these, infused with something
of her own enthusiasm and heroism, conducted the
proscribed, first one, then another, away from the
noisy, bloody arena of Paris, across the snowcapped
Juras, to the waiting silence of Coppet. She
opened her doors to friends and foes alike. In
times of need her generous heart knew no distinctions.

Once it was for a nephew of Jancourt, Achille
du Chayla, that she labored. The young man had
been arrested at a town on the frontier of Switzerland under the suspicion that the name on the
passport was not his true name, and that he was a
refugee Frenchman — a suspicion which was, of

course, correct. He was to be imprisoned until
Monsieur de Reverdil, a certain Swiss magistrate,
could see him and ascertain whether or not he were
a Frenchman. Here was a crucial case. It re-
quired all of Madame de Staël's skill and power.
She hastened to Monsieur de Reverdil, who luckily
happened to be an old family friend. She was
closeted with him a long while, arguing, entreating, demanding. Her object, of course, was to per-
suade him to save the young man by a falsehood,
to deny his French identity. Monsieur Reverdil
protested, " If I do what you ask and if the truth
be discovered, I shall no longer have the right to
claim our own countrymen when they are arrested
in France. Thus I shall jeopardize the interests
of those confided to my official care for the sake of
a man who has no legal claim on me." Madame
listened and knew that he was speaking sensibly
and justly. But all the while she was thinking of
her friend Jancourt, who was at Coppet and to
whom she desired to bring back the assurance of
his nephew's safety. She swept away all abstract
reasoning, all considerations of possible future difficulty. She sought, as she confessed, to overcome
Monsieur Reverdil's conscience by his humanity.
" If you say no," again and again she sternly
reiterated, " an only son, a man without reproach,
will be killed within twenty-four hours and your
word will have slain him." The Swiss magistrate
was finally, quite inevitably it would seem, over-

powered and vanquished. The young man was restored to his uncle. Madame de Staël rejoiced.

She was not always so successful, however. Sometimes her projects failed and she had to be a messenger of sorrow to her friends at Coppet. At such times she spoke comfort and cheer and, when these failed, a silent sympathy, more expressive than words, looked from her eyes. Many days until the Reign of Terror had passed she lived thus, mourning, helping, comforting, devoting herself, her fortune, and her home to her afflicted friends.

In this existence, tragic almost in its sombre monotony, the only interruptions were a visit to England and her mother's death. The memoirs of Fanny Burney (Madame d'Arblay) and the diary of Mrs. Phillips present interesting pictures of the English visit of the Mickleham colony and its band of exiles, of Talleyrand, the wit, of Monsieur de Narbonne, the charming, of d'Arblay, whom afterwards Fanny married, and of Madame de Staël, imperfect and lovable always.

It was not long after Madame de Staël's return from England that Madame Necker died. Mother and daughter had never fully understood each other. There had always been a something lacking in their intercourse. Yet Madame de Staël had appreciated her mother's noble character, had loved her, and now mourned. Her keenest grief, however, was in the contemplation of her father's sorrow. Between Necker and his wife, there had always existed an ideal affection and devotion. In their life together Madame de Staël had seen realized that " love in marriage " which she deemed the highest human happiness. She had looked on reverently, yearningly, sadly, knowing that she herself could never attain that happiness. Now it had passed and Necker sat with bowed head in his study. But its memory was to be to the daughter a thing beautiful and sacred, a perpetual inspiration.

During the months of the Reign of Terror Madame de Staël did not write. Before the awful drama that was being enacted in her native land, her muse stood silent and aghast, speaking only once, and then in eloquent defence of the unfortunate queen. They were months of darkness, of utter discouragement and sadness. And yet, while Madame de Staël and her companion spirits were despairing, " the period of their deliverance," to quote madame's own words, " was preparing." The ninth of Thermidor was approaching, the fall of Robespierre, and the relief of France.

Shortly after the ninth of Thermidor Madame de Staël returned to Paris. Immediately she made her appeal to the people. It was for compromise, toleration, unity. Hitherto she had been a constitutional royalist. Now she became avowedly a republican. It was one thing, she told her aristocratic friends, to oppose a republic while it was still an experiment, a thing of doubtful success, and it was quite another thing to oppose it when it was established. To overthrow the republic, she declared, and to restore the old monarchial form of government would necessitate the shedding of as much blood as had already flowed, and she revolted against the idea of further bloodshed. She wanted peace for her country, a healing, reinstating peace. Thus, above the wrangling of the factions at the capital, her voice rose pleadingly, gently, soothingly.

The liberal constitution of the year III. (1795) and the first six months of the directory found in her an eloquent supporter. And yet while she declared openly and fairly for the new government, her allegiance did not engross her to the exclusion of all other interests and sympathies. Her great magnanimous heart could not bend to any abstract theory of justice. " My political opinions," she once declared, " are proper names." There was some truth in this remark; her political opinions, while firmly founded on principle, always admitted abundant scope for consideration and care of the unfortunate. Thus it happened that, even as she took her stand on the side of the republic, across the chasm that separated her from her old-time beliefs and traditions, she extended a helping hand to her friends among the exiled nobility and clergy. She obtained the recall of Montmorency, Talleyrand, and the Abbé Montesquion.

In consequence of this diligence on behalf of the aristocrats, she was denounced from the tribune of the convention. The attack, however, was foiled by Barras, a friendly member. Again, having instigated the recall of Nupont de Nemours and certain other unpopular individuals, she was advised, somewhat threateningly, by the Committee of Public Safety to absent herself from France. Prudently, but very much against her will, she retired for a brief while.

She was soon back again in Paris and continued in her independent course, which was to unite opposites, to reconcile, so far as she was able, irreconcilables. Her salon was still hospitably open to Narbonne and Montmorency and other constitutional royalists of old time acquaintance. And once every *decade* (for thus did people persist in reckoning time, and the week had not yet reappeared) she received Benjamin Constant, Chenier, the poet, and the writers of the " Decade Philosophique." Madame de Staël was never exclusive in her social connections, but at all times liberal and broadly sympathetic, even to the point of indiscretion.

Among those who sat once every decade at her table, Benjamin Constant was the most conspicuous, the most brilliant guest. An old young man, weary of the world and its experiences, he had come to France as the one country where the novel and the unexpected might yet be found. Of course he created a sensation in the Parisian salons. With his long, fair hair, his clever, handsome face,

and his awkward grace of manner, he was, first of
all, of an unusual and attractive appearance.   Moreover, there was a distinct charm in his capricious
and tormenting personality.   Eternally logical and
cynical, without illusions and without enthusiasm,
he presented a striking contrast to the ever simple,
ardent, genial Madame de Staël.   He and she were
drawn to each other by the law of opposites, and
reacted the one upon the other, catching each
other's fires of genius, and shining all the more
brightly for their reflected lights.

Early in their intercourse, the Cercle Constitu-
tionnel was formed.   Of this republican club, which
was run counter to the royalist Club de Clichy,
Constant was the chief orator and Madame de
Staël the soul.   Their cry was for moderation.
They desired to preserve their country from the
two extremes of royalism and terrorism.   However, they lifted their voices in vain.   Their worst
fears were realized on the eighteenth of Fructidor
(Sept. 4, 1797), when the government was usurped
by the Directory and a military despotism established.   Madame de Staël had exerted her influence to obtain the appointment of Talleyrand to the
Ministry of Foreign Affairs, hoping thereby to
avert disaster.   But Talleyrand, whose selfish nature
for some unaccountable reason she had failed to
fathom, disappointed expectation, and in spite of
her earnest efforts the events of the eighteenth of
Fructidor happened.

Two years later, when on the eighteenth of Brumaire (November 9) the government passed from the hands of the Directory into those of the three Consuls, Bonaparte, Sieyes, and Roger Ducos, Madame de Staël's attitude became one of opposition. She and Constant united in a firm bond of resistance. These two, who were so dissimilar, were one in their love of liberty and hatred of tyranny. The antagonism which the despotism of the First Consul woke in both their hearts formed the final link between them. Together they raised a cry, the loudest and most triumphant in denunciation of the new government.

Madame de Staël had been favorably impressed at first with Napoleon. She recognized his greatness, and in her imagination credited him with a disinterestedness and high-mindedness which he never possessed. When she heard that he intended an invasion of Switzerland, she went to him, hoping to dissuade him from such a course. Napoleon received her graciously, listened to her patiently, but to all her arguments and pleadings he replied with talk in praise of solitude, country life, and the fine arts, for all which things, be it understood, he cared not a straw. Madame de Staël departed from his presence convinced that the eloquence of Cicero and Demosthenes combined could not move him, yet charmed against her will by his pleasant manner, his "false bonhomie." She had failed in her project, but she had learned to know the man.

He was, she determined, a person of individual purpose, indifferent to suffering, devoted to material success.

As for Napoleon's feeling toward Madame de Staël, it was hatred from the start. He liked women to be pretty toys, without opinions and without emotions. This Madame de Staël, who had such decided views on all subjects, who was so overpowering in her conversation, so energetic in her conduct, so notoriously noble and unselfish in her character, she exasperated and antagonized him. Moreover, he feared her as a dangerous rival. He was able to repress other people, but her he could not repress. She was a star whom his all-glorious and all-dazzling sunshine could not extinguish. She received in her salon the most intellectual people of the age. She inspired them with her spirit. She was the centre from which the opposition emanated.

Upon his coming to power on the eighteenth of Brumaire, Napoleon seemed desirous of winning her to his side. His brother, Joseph Bonaparte, whom Madame de Staël numbered among her friends, went to her with a question that sounded like a message from the Consul. What was it she desired, it was asked. Did she wish the two millions to be restored to her father, or residence in Paris permitted him? On both these points she should be satisfied. Then it was that she spoke those words that have become historic: " The question is not what I *want*, but what I *think*."

Protests against the growing despotism of Napoleon were proceeding from the Tribunat. Constant was the leader of the opposition, and it was a known fact that Madame de Staël applauded and even instigated him. She was by no means ignorant of the risk she ran and may have anticipated already in her thought the exile that awaited her.

On the eve of the day on which Constant was to make his celebrated speech, Madame de Staël was in her salon surrounded by her friends. Constant drew her aside and warned her that if he spoke as they had agreed that he should speak, on the morrow, her rooms would be empty, she would be deserted. Nevertheless she replied firmly: "You must obey your conscience." Often in later years, worn out with suffering, she came near to regretting that answer, yet always in her truest moments she rejoiced in it.

Constant spoke. On the same day, Madame de Staël had invited to dinner several persons whose society she said she particularly enjoyed, but who were all adherents of the new government. The dinner hour approached, but instead of guests, notes of excuse arrived. Her friends ceremoniously abandoned her, among them he whose recall from exile and whose appointment to the ministry she had obtained. Madame de Staël was not surprised, perhaps, but she was wounded, and in her most tender part, her heart.

From this time on until 1803 Madame de Staël lived alternately at Coppet and Paris. Her resistance of Napoleon's despotism was constantly forcing her away from the city, her own influence there was as constantly drawing her back again and reinstating her. She may be said to have fluctuated, with the ebb and flow of popular opinion, between the two places.

During this period Madame de Staël separated from her husband. The reason was given that the baron was a spendthrift and she wished to secure beyond his reach the fortunes of her children, August, Albert, and Albertine. The baron went out of her life without leaving any deep impression upon it. He died in 1802. Hearing of his illness, Madame de Staël went to him and nursed him and set out to take him with her to Coppet, but he died on the way thither.

Madame de Staël was at this time more than thirty years of age. Though still comparatively young, she had experienced much. She had known persecution and calumny and the falling off of friends. She had realized, too, to her sorrow, that she would never be loved with a love such as she could give. She determined, however, not to be disheartened, but to devote her life and her talents to her writing, to win by means of her pen a fame that should compensate her for what she was denied. "Let us," she wrote in a preface to one of her famous works, "stand up under the weight of existence. Let us not give our unjust enemies and our ungrateful friends the triumph of having crushed our intellectual forces. Those who would have been content with affection, they have reduced to the strife for glory. Well, then, that glory shall be won."

She had already published her book on the "Passions" and her work on "Literature," the latter in 1801. Half of Paris, out of compliment to Napoleon, had condemned what she had written, the rest had applauded, and her deserted salon was once more thronged with guests. But her three greatest triumphs, "Delphine," "Corinne," and "Germany," were still before her.

Toward the close of 1802 "Delphine" appeared. Immediately the newspapers were full of it. Every one was talking about it. Some denounced it, others were enthusiastic in their praise of it, But, while voices were disputing as to its merit, all were one in declaring that the book was a success.

The fact that many of the characters were drawn from life added to the interest of the book. People searched its pages for portraits, and found them. Delphine, it was determined, was the author herself, Madame de Staël, in her youth, with all her early illusions and hopes and sentiments; M. Labensei was Benjamin Constant idealized, so it was declared; and Madame de Vernon, it was whispered, was in feminine disguise that famous politician who had repaid Madame de Staël's many kindnesses by pleasantly and selfishly declining her invitation to dinner and thereby deserting her.

The success of "Delphine" added greatly to madame's influence. Her salon was more crowded than ever before. Even so illustrious a person as the Prince of Orange was among her guests. This was reported to Napoleon; and it was added maliciously by the informant that every rebellious word and deed which preceded from the Tribunat was known and approved by Madame de Staël. Napoleon's imperial wrath (he had recently been declared Consul for life) blazed out at the news. Formerly he had only intimated his desires that madame should betake herself into the country. This time he commanded. Madame de Staël received a letter signed by Napoleon ordering her to depart to a distance of forty leagues from Paris.

Thus began Madame de Staël's ten years of exile. Forced to leave France, Madame de Staël turned her steps to Germany. She travelled thither in company with Constant (who was also exiled) and her three children. A new sphere had opened out before her. Hitherto, by choice she had confined herself to Paris and the Parisian people. Henceforth she was to make the continent her stage and all the people of Europe her audience. Her mind, coming within range of the great minds of other countries, was to broaden and receive additional force and inspiration.

Yet, spite of the many splendors of the new and vast field on which she had entered, Madame de Staël, while glorying in these splendors, sighed yearningly for the little plot of home territory that was forbidden ground. Launched in eloquent praise of Germany, its enlightenment, its culture, and its institutions, she would break off abruptly. " Oh, for a morsel of France!" she would exclaim. She spoke of her travels as a continuous chain, of which one end was Paris and the other her heart.

In Germany Madame de Staël visited Berlin and Weimar and made the acquaintance of Goethe, Schiller, Heine, Schlegel, and the German princes. Goethe admired her against his will. Schiller found her the most talkative and the most intellectual of women, and complained with a delightful mingling of pathos and humor that the devil had sent " the French female philosopher " to torment him just in the middle of his new play. Heine described her as " a whirlwind in petticoats." And Schlegel comprehended her, appreciated her, and made himself her friend.

A sad event, perhaps the saddest in her life, recalled Madame de Staël from Germany and brought her back to Coppet. Her father, who was the one dearest to her in the world, died. At a much

later day, when madame herself was dying, she
spoke thus to a friend : "I have always been the
same intense and sorrowful. I have loved God,
my father, and liberty." Grave, beautiful words,
they reveal her soul in all its strength, simplicity,
and fervor. From them we know the place her
father held in her affections and may realize what
losing him meant to her. One of Necker's last
acts had been to plead with Napoleon (fruitlessly,
of course) for his daughter. "It was the last
time," wrote Madame de Staël, "that his protecting hand was extended over my life."

Madame de Staël passed her season of first
mourning in editing her father's works. In 1804
she set out with August Schlegel and her three
children for Italy. Here, for the first time, under
the bluest of skies and the tutorship of Schlegel,
she made the acquaintance of the fine arts. Here
she conversed with the Roman princes, was made
an Arcadian Academician and had "endless son-
nets" written to her. And here, too, she dreamed,
and conceived that poetic "Corinne," which was
later to be born to the world of literature.

Immediately upon her return to Switzerland,
Madame de Staël began to write "Corinne." As
she drew near to its close, her homesickness for
Paris became intense. When her attention was
called to the beauty of Leman, she could only turn
away her face and sigh. "Oh, for the stream of
the Rue du Bac!" she exclaimed. The Rue du

Bac flowed near her city residence, and once, when a friend with whom she was walking paused to admire the view, "So," she observed, "still prejudiced in favor of the country!" And then, perceiving that she had said something surprising, she smiled apologetically. Thus she was continually disclosing her lack of appreciation of nature and her absorbing passion for society, conversation, and the haunts of men, especially for all these things as they existed in Paris.

At length the magnet proving irresistible and Fouchet, the chief of police, whose policy it was to do "as little needless harm as possible," condescending to shut one eye, she shortened the proscribed distance to eighteen leagues and established herself at Acosta. Here she received her friends, and read the proof-sheets of her book, and occasionally ventured stealthily, by the light of the stars, within the bounds of her beloved city. Her sincere emotion got the better of her dignity. And yet, do we love her any the less for this?

In 1807 Corinne was published. It was welcomed by all Europe and enthusiastically praised. It gave to the world of literature one more immortal character, one more love song that men would not forget. In Corinne, as in Delphine, people recognized Madame de Staël. "Corinne is Delphine," wrote the poet Chenier, "Delphine matured and acting under the twofold inspiration of genius and love."

Of course, the ruler of France was incensed by this new triumph of his rival. A scathing criticism of the book, which appeared shortly after its publication, in the columns of the Moniteur, was reported to have been written by his imperial hand. A new decree of punishment followed. Madame de Staël was once more driven back to Coppet.

Coppet, the brilliant, the regal, the inspired! Although Madame de Staël turned her steps thither so reluctantly and fretted against her residence there like a prisoner against his iron bar, nevertheless it was at Coppet that she appeared in her full majesty and at her best, and it is at Coppet that imagination likes best to place her.

At Coppet she was always surrounded by a court that represented the talent, wit, beauty, birth, and intellect of Europe. Among the most frequent of her visitors were Constant and Schlegel, Sismondi and Bonstetten, the famous beauty, Madame Récamier, with whom all the world was in love, and the priestess who had once been so notorious a coquette, Madame de Krüdner.

The world at Coppet had its various moods. Sometimes it was serious and philosophic; then words flew among the company like arrows, a very rain of them, pointed, swift, and sure, and never did arrows make more dazzling flights than the winged words of Constant and Madame de Staël. Sometimes, again, the world at Coppet was merely gay, enjoyment was the order of the day; then plays were acted, often classics, but oftener comedies and tragedies written by the hostess or one of the guests. And finally the world at Coppet was sometimes fractious and had its quarrellings and makings-up. Beneath the trees, beside the lake, love was declared and hearts were broken and enduring friendships were formed.

In the world of Coppet, so Arcadian, so Edenlike if we do not seek to study it too long or too closely, there were occasional storms. All was not calm and pleasant between Constant and Madame de Staël. They were continually accusing each other, apologizing, and making promises. Constant desired to marry Madame de Staël. She, however, would only consent to a secret marriage, and he would have none but an open one. Madame Récamier was the peace-maker between them. She reconciled them to each other, and then they quarrelled again. Finally, in 1808, Constant himself put an end to all these complications and perplexities by marriage with another woman.

Toward the close of 1807 Madame de Staël left Coppet and made a second visit to Germany. She stayed there collecting material for a book on Germany which she was planning to write. She returned to Coppet in the fall of 1808 and straightway entered upon her new work. For two years she labored steadily in the composition of this, her longest and most arduous literary production. As

soon as she had completed it she established herself
at Blois for the sake of correcting the proof-sheets
as they issued from the press.

The story of the suppression of the book, culmi-
nating act of Napoleon's cruelty, is well-known.
The literary censors seized it on the very eve of its
publication. The sheets were sent to the paste-
board maker and were destroyed, and the authoress
was commanded to leave Paris within three days
for Coppet. The book was not published until
three years later, 1813, when it appeared in England and was the event of the season.

Madame de Staël's bitterness on the occasion of
the suppression of her book may be imagined.
Her time and labor wasted and oppression redoubled
when she was beginning to hope for reconciliation!
One does not wonder that her great heart sank
under this added weight of persecution.

Her marriage to Monsieur Rocca, which occurred
at this time, served in a measure to lighten the
burden. Madame de Staël had always longed for
love. Not many knew this. The world in general
believed her all mind. Some few, however, such
as Byron, divined in her the presence of an unseen
force, a deep, emotional nature. Her marriage
with Rocca, a young man twenty years her junior,
revealed her secret at a late and (as society judged)
at an untimely date. Her own mature age and
Rocca's wounds and failing health gave to this
tardy happiness an air of sadness.

The year 1811, following the suppression of her Germany and preceding her flight, was a hard year, indeed one might almost say the hardest year, for Madame de Staël. Then no longer her "motif" rippled, even for a moment, lightly, brightly in the treble key. It sounded now only in those sombre chords, those final harmonies that were to introduce the noble funeral march. Her youth, in which she had rejoiced so fondly, was gone. Friends were cooling, darkening towards her, and deserting her. Others, the true, were made to suffer for her sake. Madame Récamier and Mathieu de Montmorency were banished from France in consequence of a visit which they paid her. Schlegel, accountably for no other reason than his faithfulness to her, was ordered to leave Coppet. More than all else Madame de Staël lamented this striking down of her devoted friends. " I am the Orestes of exile," she declared, sorrowfully

At this point, this crisis in her vicissitudes, the prefect of Geneva came to her and suggested that she write something in honor of Napoleon's son, the little king of Rome, and thereby instate herself in favor. She replied unhesitatingly with one of those brilliant flashes of repartee that so illuminated her discourse. " All I desire for the child is a good nurse," she said. Her love of liberty, her indomitable spirit, never faltered and, though so sorely pressed, she would not stoop to propitiate her persecutor by one word of praise.

Meanwhile, to Madame de Staël Europe had become a prison. She studied its map; planning whither she should make her escape. She determined upon England. But so closely was she watched, so restricted was she in her movements, that she was forced to travel thither stealthily by way of Brussels and Sweden. She stayed in England until the happy time when the abdication of Napoleon and the Restoration opened the gates of Paris to her. Then, once more her eager footsteps were treading the dear, familiar streets.

She brought to the capital, with her, politics that were no longer republican. The English constitution had taken possession of her mind. She returned to that liberal royalism of opinion that she had professed in her youthful days beneath her father's roof. She was weary of the political turmoil through which France had been passing and desired for her country a system mild, "homelike," and old fashioned.

During the all too brief term of life that remained to her, Madame de Staël resumed her old ways. Once more she held court in her Parisian salon and received there as in former days LaFayette, Lally Tollendal, Montmorency, even the faithless Talleyrand. In Madame de Staël's generous soul there was no place for rancor, and she welcomed friends and forgave offenders with an indiscriminate cordiality of spirit.

Her last days were made pleasant for her by the

happy marriage of her daughter Albertine, the noble career of her eldest son August, and the devotion of her young husband. Her friends, too, many of whom had estranged themselves from her, gathered affectionately about her again. At her side appeared the faces of Montmorency, Sismondi, Constant, and the dear Juliette (Madame Rècamier), and her celebrated lover, Chateaubriand. For the last time the " dark, magnificent " eyes smiled upon them and the eloquent lips spoke final words of comfort and love.

All Europe mourned the death of Madame de Staël. Many funeral tributes were rendered to her in many places and at many times. Of these none, perhaps, was more touching and sincere than the visit paid by Madame Rècamier and Chateaubriand to her home, of which Chateaubriand has told us. Fifteen years had passed since the death of Madame de Staël when he and Madame Rècamier together made their pilgrimage to Coppet.

The chateau was deserted, but memories everywhere met Madame Rècamier, and she communed with them silently, viewing those spots where Madame de Staël had played the piano, and talked, and written. With her lover at her side, she wandered out into the park and, not wishing to display her grief, she parted from him and went alone to the grave. The figure of the weeping Juliette and that of her melancholy companion at the gate, the mountains, the lake, and the " clouds of gold spreading like a glory above a bier " present a picture impressive and memorable.   It serves as a fitting and final monument to the genius of the most famous of famous French women, Madame de Staël.

MADAME RÉCAMIER.

Born in Lyons, Dec. 4, 1777.
Died in Paris, May 11, 1849.

"Beloved always and by all from the cradle to the grave."
— *Madame d'Hautefenille.*

IT was referred to tenderly, reverently as "the little cell." Without, the sun set over the hills of Sèvres, and slender church spires touched the sky, and nuns walked in the quiet convent garden and pupils played beneath the shade of the acacia trees. Within there were books and pictures, a piano and a harp. Flower-pots stood in the windows and birds perched on the blinds. And over all was an atmosphere of mystery, of seclusion, of distinction. Those who climbed the stairs and crossed the threshold did so with a certain uplift of the spirit and a softening of voice. They came to the cell as to a sanctuary.

One finds it difficult to apply to the little cell the name of salon. Yet such it was. Situated in the Abbaye-aux-Bois at a remote end of Paris, it could not have been more retired. Yet fashion found it out and made its way there. No spot was more visited. There Gerard came to show his pictures, Lamartine to read his "Meditations,"

and Delphine Gay to recite her verses. Of various
talents, ranks, and parties, they assembled from all
quarters. Conspicuous among them were Benjamin
Constant and Ballanche, the philosopher, Matthieu
de Montmorency, M. J. J. Ampère, Eugene Dela-
croix, David d' Angers, Augustin Périer, Monsieur
Bertin, and he who was crowned king over all,
Chateaubriand. It was a little world, select and
yet inclusive, that travelled daily to the Abbaye-aux-
Bois. It mingled its life, its sparkle, with the
shadows of the convent. And thus it may be
said the little cell became a sort of half-way house
between the two extremes of worldliness and other
worldliness.

Of course there was the magnet, the dweller in
the little cell, she who by the law of irresistible
attraction drew society with her into her seclusion.
She had already reached the period of the " much
dreaded forties." Yet she was still " Juliette,"
the fair, the incomparable, the best beloved woman
in France.

Perhaps you went to see her prejudiced against
her, incredulous of that charm of which you had
heard so much. She was only a pretty coquette,
you told yourself. She had done more harm than
good in the world. She was admired merely because she was the fashion. You were determined
that she should not captivate you. You climbed
the narrow stairway, you stood on the threshold
of the little cell. A woman of dark, curling hair,

MADAME RÉCAMIER.
From a painting by David in the Louvre.

of brilliant eyes, and a wonderful radiance of complexion came toward you. She spoke your name,
she greeted you. Immediately you felt that you
had stepped within the circle of kindness and
benevolence. She asked you a few questions not
with politeness only, but with a real and undis-
guised interest. You answered and she listened
with a smile that said, " I understand." You
grew eloquent, you outdid yourself, you talked
as you had never talked before. You were pleased
with yourself, with every one about you, and most
of all with her against whom you had previously
been so determined. Thus the work of conquest
was accomplished. You *came*, you *saw*, but invari-
ably it was she who *conquered*.

It is at the Abbaye-aux-Bois that imagination
likes best to place Madame Récamier. There,
divested of youth and fortune and the first flush of
her radiant beauty, she appears in a softened and
poetic light. There, too, her goodness, unchanged
by circumstance, rises to a height that has been
termed "celestial." Never before has she occupied
a place so important and so lofty. It is there that
she seems most fitly to belong.

Nevertheless, the period of her youth, of her first
conquests and early indiscretions is not without
its interest and glamor. The record of that time
reads very like a mythical tale, a chapter of romance. All the good fairies seem to have been
present at her birth and to have bestowed upon her

gifts of fortune more plentiful even than her names.
And her names certainly were not few. Jeanne
François Julie Adelaide Bernard she was christened. In thinking of her, however, in addressing
her, it was only the name Julie that was remembered, Julie transformed into Juliette. It was the
name that best suited her. She was most unmis-
takably a Juliette, and a Juliette whose Romeo
was never far away.

Even in her pretty childhood she was not without her Romeo. In such rare glimpses as we have
of her playing beside the bright waters of the *Loire*
or climbing a tree to pick the grapes that grew in
a neighbor's garden, we see her never unattended.
There is always at her side some ardent young
squire.

Yet it was no youthful gallant who, while she
was yet a child, won her hand in marriage. It was
instead a middle-aged gentleman, a friend of her
parents. Among the guests who were received by
Monsieur and Madame Bernard in their house in
Paris, whither, on monsieur's appointment as col-
lector of customs, they had repaired, was a former
citizen of theirs, Monsieur Récamier. He was a
wealthy banker, affable and courtly. When he and
Juliette were married he was forty-two and she
fifteen. The tie between them was never anything
but nominal and his attitude to her was always
one of paternal fondness and indulgence.

It was in the period of the Consulate that Madame

Récamier, all-dazzling and all-enchanting, made her début. She was immediately admired, surrounded, courted. There was danger in the world which she entered, a danger like fire. In her innocence and fearlessness she played with the fire, she revelled in the danger. Yet she never descended from her high altitude or came into too close contact with the flames. Among the gifts which the good fairies had bestowed upon her was a triumphant purity.

We have spoken of the good fairies who visited Juliette. We must not forget a certain naughty little fairy. It is now time to mention her. It was she who gave to Juliette the spirit of coquetry. People are forever trying to excuse this coquetry. Madame de Staël called it "benevolent," and Sainte Beuve characterized it as "angelic." It had indeed, paradoxical as it may seem, something of a sweet and soothing character. Without a thought of harming any one, the lovely Juliette shot her arrows; they always hit, and when she saw she had inflicted wounds, she hastened to apply the balm of friendship. It was marvellous, the way in which she converted lovers into friends. She did not extinguish the passions she inspired. Rather she tempered them. She did not lead one from the tropics to the snows, but to that mild and temperate zone which she inhabited and which was not without its sunshine and its flowers.

Thus Madame Récamier was "benevolent" in her coquetry, she was "angelic." Yet those who excuse her have to censure her as well. She could not heal all whom she wounded. Some, it is said, remained incurably hardened and embittered. And we are reminded of women, her unfortunate rivals, wives, and sweethearts neglected for her sake. They appear never to have accused her. Yet they must have had, many of them, their heartaches, which they endured in silence.

All this reveals what Sainte Beuve calls "the dark side" in the character of Madame Récamier. It was a darkness which, in her later days, she herself realized and regretted. She found the explanation and punishment in a fate that excluded her from all the close affections of domestic life. Married to a man who was her father rather than her husband, she lived what may be termed a solitary existence. No one was so admired, so loved, so féted as she, yet no one was more alone. Sometimes she turned from her triumphs and her conquests to weep a few tears in longing for the happiness that was denied her. Ballanche, her loyal friend, who understood her so perfectly, was right in likening her to the phœnix. She "fed on perfumes" and "lived in the purest regions of the air, yet envied the humble fate of the white dove because she had a companion like herself."

In the absence of home ties it was in friendship that Madame Récamier found her pleasure and consolation, one might almost say her vocation. It was to friendship that she devoted herself faithfully, zealously, unselfishly. She was never known to abandon any one to whom she had once given her affection. Her loyalty, Madame de Staël said, was like " the spring in the desert."

She was equally the friend of men and women, beloved by both. Madame de Staël, Madame de Genlis, Madame de Krüdner, Madame de Swetchine, innumerable other mesdames, were extravagant in their praise of her. Moreover, it is a significant fact, that which has been observed before, that the wives of her admirers spoke no word of envy or detraction against her. Some even were on intimate terms with her. Madame de Montmorency, after her husband's death, gave her own letters from him to Madame Récamier, as a mark of her confidence and esteem. And Madame de Chateaubriand, whenever Madame Récamier was reported to be leaving town, hastened to her, imploring her to return as soon as possible. " What is to become of Monsieur de Chateaubriand?" She would inquire anxiously. " What is he going to do if you stay away long?" Thus these French wives accepted her, courted her. Posterity can only wonder — and smile.

It was reasons of friendship that drew Madame Récamier into the opposition and brought upon her the ban of exile. Before the execution of the Duke d' Enghein, General Moreau's trial, and the persecution of Madame de Staël, she preserved a neutral attitude. Fouché, finding her beautiful

and charming and therefore powerful, conceived
the idea of attaching her to the government. He
wished to make her one of the maids of honor.
Madame Récamier excused herself on the plea of
her shyness and her love of independence. Her
refusal angered Fouché.

This, however, did not happen until after her
meeting with Napoleon. The First Consul saw
her at the house of his sister, Madame Bacciocchi,
and admired her. She was then residing outside
of Paris, at Clichy. Lucien, the brother of the
Consul, was at that time foolishly, hopelessly, and
passionately in love with her. He also was at
Madame Bacciocchi's. He chanced to be standing
at Madame Récamier's side. The Consul, who was
in Lucien's secret, noticed them together. He
passed them and, as he did so, looking meaningly
at Madame Récamier, he took occasion to whisper
audibly in his brother's ear, "And I, too, would like
to go to Clichy." At dinner, the place at Napoleon's left had been intended for Madame Récamier; but through a misunderstanding she did not
take it. The Second Consul, Cambacères, seated
himself beside her. Napoleon, observing, declared
loudly, "Ha! Ha! citizen Consul, always next to
the most beautiful." After dinner he accosted
Madame Récamier, "Why did you not take the
seat next to me?" he inquired. "I should not
have presumed," she replied. "It was your place,"
he told her.

Thus, at first, Madame Récamier enjoyed Napoleon's favor. Later, when she refused to serve at his court and, by her friendship for the victims of his despotism, allied herself with the opposition, he turned his enmity against her.

The ministers of his cabinet and visiting princes were obliged to make their calls on Madame Récamier stealthily so as to escape the emperor's displeasure. Once, when news was brought him that three of his ministers had encountered one another by chance at her house, he inquired with forbidding irony, "How long is it since the council have met at Madame Récamier's?" And again, when she lost her fortune and all of France extended its sympathy to her, he remarked testily, "They could not have paid more honor to the widow of a marshal of France who had lost her husband on the field of battle."

All this occurred during the Empire. But at even an earlier date, under the Consulate, Madame Récamier had been made to feel Napoleon's power. Monsieur Bernard, her father, who was in the post-office department, was compromised. He was imprisoned at Napoleon's orders and threatened with death. Madame Récamier learned this, suddenly, while she was entertaining friends at dinner. Madame Bacciocchi, the sister of Napoleon, was among the guests present. She advised Madame Récamier to see Fouché and promised that she herself would do all she could for Monsieur Bernard.

Madame Récamier, therefore, attempted an interview with Fouché; but he refused to receive her, for fear, he said, of being influenced by her in an affair of state. She then sought Madame Bacciocchi at the Theâtre-Français. Madame Bacciocchi was there, occupying a box with her sister Pauline. There was a gentleman with them. The play was Achilles and the actor Lafont. Madame Récamier, troubled and agitated, entered the box. The two sisters seemed not to notice her suffering. Madame Bacciocchi observed indifferently that she wished to remain until the end of the tragedy, and Pauline, absorbed in the play, remarked that she thought the helmet very unbecoming to Lafont. At this the gentleman, General Bernadotte it was, came forward. He offered to escort Madame Récamier to her home and then, himself, to see Napoleon. Thus began Bernadotte's attachment to Madame Récamier. He interceded for her, and saved her father, received her very gracious gratitude and became thenceforth one of her most devoted Romeos.

This instance was Madame Récamier's first experience of Napoleon's power. Her final experience was her exile. Upon the suppression of Madame de Staël's "Germany," Madame Récamier determined to go to Coppet and pay a visit of sympathy to her sorrowing friend. She was counselled not to go. She was told that she could do her friend no good and that she would only be bringing misfortune upon herself. But she persisted. What she intended doing was only natural and right, she said, and whatever might be the consequences she was resolved not to refuse to a persecuted woman this mark of respect and affection. She went to Coppet and embraced Madame de Staël and was, in consequence, banished to a distance of forty leagues from Paris.

Much has been said in contempt of the friendship of women. Yet here is one that defies carping criticism. Madame Récamier's love for Madame de Staël, her unselfish devotion to her, form one of the pleasantest chapters in the lives of both. Madame de Staël, on her part, was equally loving. She delighted to see her beautiful Juliette admired and courted, receiving as she declared "the worship of the whole of Europe." She regarded her as the chief attraction at Coppet during those seasons when Madame Récamier made her visits there. "I cannot conceive of either country or home life without you," she once told her. "Everything falls to pieces when you leave. You are the sweet and tranquil centre of our home."

Perhaps no chapter in Madame Récamier's life is more pleasant, more gratifying, than this one devoted to her friendship with Madame de Staël. But there are other chapters given to other friends which have their individual importance and charm. We might say of these other chapters that they are

romantic chapters. One is found entitled Lucien,
another Bernadotte. Then follow the Montmorencies, Prince Augustus of Prussia, Ballanche,
Canova, Benjamin Constant, and last and chiefest,
Chateaubriand.

We have already had a peep into those that treat
of Lucien and Bernadotte. Next in order are the
Montmorencies, the cousins Matthieu and Adrien.
Of these, Matthieu was the saint. He was Madame
Récamier's mentor. He reproved her for her frivolity and love of admiration and tried to direct her
thoughts to more serious things and especially to
heaven. For his sake she gave an hour every day
to meditation and religious reading. Adrien, who
became Duke de Laval, was quite different from
Matthieu. He was less of a saint and more of a
wit. He, his father, and later his son, all loved
Madame Récamier. Thus three generations rendered homage to her. Adrien used frequently to
meet his son at Madame Récamier's. On such
occasions, the father and son, rivals *per force*, each
endeavored, as the vulgar saying is, "to sit the
other out." It was the younger man who invari-
ably persisted longest, and the duke wrathfully
took his departure. Nevertheless, the humor of
the situation did not escape the duke, and he wrote
of it very pleasantly to Madame Récamier: "My
son is enchanted with you. You know whether or
not I am. It is the same with all the Montmorencies. We do not die, but we are all of us wounded."

Of all the romantic chapters in the life of Madame Récamier assuredly the one of most poetic glamor is that with Prince Augustus of Prussia. It had for its setting Coppet, the beautiful shores of Lake Geneva, and the mystic grandeur of Mt. Blanc, and for its hero a brave and handsome young prince. Madame Récamier was twenty-five and the prince twenty-four when they met at Coppet. He was immediately her captive, " a royal prisoner." His boyish ardor, his earnestness, his perfect sincerity touched Madame Récamier. And the glory of his name and rank and valorous deeds appealed to her imagination. The prince, who was a Protestant, proposed to Madame Récamier that she should break a tie that had never been anything but nominal and marry him. Madame Récamier wavered. She wrote to her husband asking for a divorce. She received in answer a tender, fatherly, dignified letter. It aroused Madame Récamier's compassion for her husband. She pictured him old and stripped of his fortune, lonely and sad. She determined not to desert him. But she did not tell Prince Augustus of her decision. She could not bear to deprive him of all hope and allowed matters with him to drift on in sweet and poetic uncertainty. He left her dreaming of the happiness of a life with her, believing that it might be realized. She let him go thus, thinking that time and absence would be his best helps to an understanding of the truth. It was a naïve philosophy and one that has called forth much criticism of Madame Récamier. One wonders if frankness would not have been more salutary in the end.

Shortly after her return to Paris, she sent the prince her portrait. He sat for hours, he told her, looking at "the enchanting picture" and thinking that no fate could be comparable to that of the man whom she would love. He did not part with the portrait until his death, many years after. Madame Récamier had also presented him with a ring. Three months before his death he wrote concerning it: "The ring that you gave me I shall carry with me to the tomb."

After the chapter with Prince Augustus, the next in sequence is one with Ballanche. Madame Récamier met him at Lyons, whither she went in her exile. He used to call every evening and chat with her tête-à-tête. They talked of his work and of ethical and literary subjects. Shy and ugly, the philosopher had never met with such tact and kindness as that which he received from Madame Récamier. He was full of gratitude and admiration. He became to her an ideal sort of elder brother, loving her, caring for her, following her everywhere with a watchful devotion. It was he who advised her to translate Petrarch. More to please him than from any belief in her own ability she began the work. It was laid aside and taken up again many times. She died before it was completed.

When Madame Récamier left Lyons for Italy, Ballanche visited her there. Canova made a third in their little excursions. And with Canova we enter upon another romantic chapter. Upon her arrival at Rome one of Madame Récamier's first calls had been at the sculptor's studio. He, who was a passionate lover of beauty, did not fail to honor it in Madame Récamier. During the summer months, when residence in the city was unhealthful, Madame Récamier became Canova's guest at Albano. There her room looked out upon the Campagna, Pompey's villa surrounded by trees, a vast plain of waving green grass, and, as a limit of all this, the sea. Every morning she walked on the shores of Lake Albano, and every Sunday at high mass and vespers she played the organ in the little church. She was *la belissima Zulieta* of the place. While she was in Italy Madame Récamier visited Naples. When she returned to Rome, Canova met her with a cordial and affectionate greeting and with an air of mystery as well. He led her to his private "atelier" and drew aside a curtain. "See if I have not thought of you," he said. Two clay busts were disclosed, both of Madame Récamier, one veiled and the other unveiled.

At the very first of the new era of the Restoration Madame Récamier left Italy and returned to Paris. It is to this period (1814–15) that the chapter that has to do with Benjamin Constant

belongs. The king and queen of Italy, Monsieur
and Madame Murat, friends of Madame Récamier,
desired a defender of their rights in the congress
that was to determine the new balance of power.
Madame Récamier bethought her of Benjamin
Constant and determined to interview him in
behalf of the Murats. He was already something
of an old friend. She had known him for ten
years. She went, intent to please him, and she
succeeded only too well. The interview was the
beginning of a foolish passion on the part of Benjamin Constant which never received the least encouragement. All through the winter, however,
for reasons of policy, Madame Récamier saw much
of "the publicist." He and she both of them
occasionally attended Madame Krüdner's semi-
social, semi-spiritualistic meetings. Madame
Récamier's arrival at these gatherings was thought
to divert attention from the solemn business of the
occasion. Therefore Constant was requested to
address her on this score. The note that resulted
is an excellent example of the brilliant, aerial mind
of her volatile lover. "Madame Krüdner has just
charged me with an embarrassing commission," he
wrote. "She begs that you will make your appearance with as few charms as possible. She
says that you dazzle everybody and consequently
all hearts are disturbed, attention is impossible.
You cannot divest yourself of your beauty; but,
prithee, do not enhance it."

With the exit of Benjamin Constant we approach the final romantic chapter, that of which Chateaubriand is the hero. Madame Récamier met Chateaubriand first at the house of Madame de Staël and again several years after, near the time of Madame de Staël's death, at her house again. Her intimate friendship with him, however, was not until the days at the Abbaye-aux-Bois.

It was during the last years of the Restoration that Madame Récamier met with her second reverse of fortune and in consequence removed to the little cell. She lived there for six months. At the end of that time the nuns ceded to her a suite of rooms on the first floor of the Abbaye, and there she remained until very shortly before her death.

During the time of her residence at the Abbaye-aux-Bois Madame Récamier ceased to be young. She did not grow old; in spite of the years she attained, she never grew old. Her heart was perpetually young, perpetually beautiful. And though the passage of time divested her somewhat of her charms, she submitted herself so gracefully that she was permitted to retain more than she lost. The smile was always the same, and the graceful carriage, and the sweet, charitable manner. Her coquetry, too, that desire, that power of pleasing, remained with her. It had developed since the days of her youthful flirtations. It never wounded now — it only healed. It consisted in recognizing and honoring every talent, every virtue, every distinction and in addressing itself equally to the most obscure and the most celebrated. It was the soul of kindness and courtesy.

Of the influence that Madame Récamier exerted at this time Sainte Beuve, who knew her, has written. Hers was a "benevolent" power, he said. She brought "the art of friendship" to perfection. She disarmed anger, sweetened bitterness, and banished rudeness. She instituted the reign of compassion and indulgence. She doctored the faults and the weaknesses of her friends as she would have doctored their physical infirmities. She was, Sainte Beuve concludes, a veritable "Sister of Charity."

She admitted many to her fireside and to her heart. She was general in her friendship. Yet she was special, too. And Chateaubriand was her specialty. For him she remained in the city and surrounded herself with friends. For him she devised musical entertainments, readings of his own works, anything that would amuse him. She brought admirers to his feet, smiles to his melancholy countenance. She watched his face and anticipated his every wish. She flattered his humors, she lightened his gloom, she filled his life.

Every day at half past two she received him in her little salon. Together they drank tea and enjoyed an hour of tête-à-tête.

The years went by. Monsieur de Chateaubriand met with an accident that crippled him for life. In his journeys to the Abbaye-aux-Bois he had to be carried to and from his carriage. Madame Récamier grew ill, her eyesight failed. Yet they continued to meet at the old hour. It had become a necessity with them.

When his wife died, Monsieur de Chateaubriand asked Madame Récamier, who had long been a widow, to honor his name by consenting to bear it. But Madame Récamier shook her head. " Let us change nothing in so perfect an affection," she said. And to her friends she remarked, " If he were married to me, Monsieur de Chateaubriand would miss his morning call."

Thus the final chapter draws to an end, and it is time to close the volume. A last look shows us Madame Récamier in her cloistered retreat. Let us take leave of her there in the shadow of the convent, surrounded by the friends who loved her. Her life had been long, but her star had not grown dim.

MADAME VALMORE.

Born at Douai, June 20, 1789.
Died in Paris, June 23, 1859.

'Sweet spirit with the golden voice." — *Brizeux.*

AMID the dust and defilement of the city this
bird of plaintive note built her nest. On dizzy
heights, now the fifth floor, now the sixth floor of
some humble lodging-house, it swung. The storms
visited it and buffetted it and overturned it, and
another bough as dry and leafless as the former
was sought, and the nest was built again. Yet the
sunshine found it, too; and the cries of the unfortunate were lifted to it, never in vain.

Within the little nest Madame Valmore worked
and loved and prayed. And she sang, too, repeatedly, inevitably. She sang of sad, far-away memories, of present needs and present pains, of the
prisoner, the exile, the bereft. She sang with tears
in her voice and grief in her heart. "She was,"
Sainte Beuve declares, "the Mater Dolorosa of
poetry."

She did not live alone in the little nest. She
had with her her family, four dear companions, —
Valmore, her husband, who was honor itself, but
who vainly sought for honest and congenial employment, and three children, Hippolyte, her son,

254

MADAME VALMORE.
From an etching by Monziès.

and Undine and Inez, her daughters. Hippolyte was a good boy. His fine mind and his straightforward nature were a great comfort to his mother. Inez, the baby of the family, was sensitive and shy, inclined to melancholy. "No child," her mother said, "ever needed so much caressing." She was frail, too, a constant anxiety to her mother. Sunshine, fresh air, comfort, pleasure, were what she needed. But though her mother worked early and late, and longed with all her heart to buy them for her, they could not be bought. The child grew every year more delicate and spirit-like. Undine was only occasionally an inmate of the little nest. She was assistant teacher in a boarding-school at Chaillot, and could pay only fleeting visits to her home. It was as "our dear learned lady" that Madame Valmore spoke of her. She came and went before her mother's eyes like some fair vision not wholly realized and understood. Small of stature, with soft blue eyes, regular features, and a sweet winning smile, there was, it has been stated, something angelic in her appearance. She was a poet like her mother, and lived in a world of dreams and pure and lofty thoughts. But she was reserved and undemonstrative. Her reticence troubled her mother. Madame Valmore, who opened her heart so freely to all who loved her, experienced an affectionate alarm when her daughter's confidence was withheld from her. But she did not question Undine unduly. She respected her silence. She was always considerate of the wishes of her children. " These sensitive young souls need either happiness or the dream of it," she said, " and should be fed from the first on unalterable indulgence."

For herself she had ceased to ask for happiness. Sometimes, it is true, she sighed for rest and the modest luxury of an apartment on the second floor. But oftener she spoke of her supports and comforts, — the daylight, faith in God, the love of her dear ones, and the hope of seeing again those who had " gone before her." The truth was she no longer expected or desired happiness save that of others.

Her days from eight o'clock till midnight were filled with work, letters, housekeeping, sewing, visitors. She made her life, she declared, as she sewed, patiently, "stitch by stitch." She did what she could for the maintenance of her poor little home. She labored " with all her might." Yet when they came asking her to write stories for papers and periodicals, she shook her head. " I cannot write," she said. " My thoughts are too serious, my heart too full. I always write from the heart, and mine bleeds too much for pretty, childish fancies."

People, charmed by her plaintive bird-notes, climbed to her attic heights to visit her. They came, litterateurs, and now and then a stray prince or princess. Madame Valmore received them with ease and grace and hospitality. She surrounded herself with an artistic poverty, made light of her too apparent needs, and hid her sorrows under a gallant bearing. She who was so modest and sensitive a poet was also proud and brave.

The rich man came to tell her of his troubles. The house that he was building was to have cost a hundred thousand francs, he said, and the plans were mounting up to twice that sum, which, together with the cost of his son's education, was enough to drive him mad. Madame was forced to pity him. Yet she smiled to herself ironically as she listened. "What can you say to such a child of fortune?" she inquired of a friend. "That you have but two chemises and no tablecloths?" He would reply, "Ah, how fortunate you are! Then you will not think of building."

Two noble ladies came to take her for a drive. They cast a glance of scrutiny about the narrow quarters. "Madame Valmore has everything so pretty around her," they remarked. And Madame Valmore, while she thanked them for their compliment, thought of the one franc lying in her bureau drawer, which was all she had saved toward the monthly wages of "the fierce Victoire." She could not go with the great ladies to drive. She must stay at home and work. But for excuse she only said that she was ill. Thus, as in the days of her dramatic career, she hid her tears beneath the jester's mask.

Her lot was cast in the shadow, away from the
pleasures of the world. She did not know happiness. She had never known it. Of herself she
said that she "slipped sorrowfully into the world."

There is something very sad, very sweet, and
very affecting about Madame Valmore's first memories and her early home at Douai. In that town,
so quaint, so historic, so picturesque, so permeated
with Flemish and Spanish influences, while the bells
were ringing in the Revolution, near to a grave-
yard and a ruined church on the Rue Notre Dame,
Madame Valmore was born. She played among
the tombstones and the fallen statues of the saints;
she gathered the roses that grew wild along the
ancient aisles and cloisters; she gazed upon the picture of the Christ, and it seemed to her that the
eyes looked down on her in pity.

The little Marceline, as she was called, could
not remember ever having been anything but poor.
Her brother Felix, however, and her sisters Cecile
and Eugenie, who were older than she, were able
to think back to a time before the Revolution,
when the church was still standing and when there
was plenty in their home. Then there father had
been an armorial painter. But in the days that
followed, when royalty was swept away, his occu-
pation vanished. To be sure there were wealthy
Protestant uncles in Flanders who promised business opportunities and preferment if they would
but change their faith. But the family in the Rue

Notre Dame were devout Catholics. They remained loyal and poor.

When Marceline was ten years old she went with her mother to Guadeloupe, whither they had been invited by a relative who had amassed a fortune. They had not been there long when the mother caught the yellow fever, which was raging there, and died. The relative was already dead of the fever. Marceline was quite alone. She was befriended by the wife of a ship owner, Madame Geudon. When she was fourteen she took passage on a ship of Madame Geudon's husband that was sailing for France. On her way she encountered a storm. She persuaded the sailors to let her remain on deck while it was raging, and, tightly wrapped in the shrouds, she watched the battle with the waves. The fierce beauty of the scene appealed to her dramatic and poetic nature. She faced it with that same dauntless spirit with which she was to face all the later conflicts of her life.

On her landing in France, Marceline was met with the news that her family was destitute. It was then that she became an actress. Young, small, innocent-looking, without mannerisms or affectations, quick, simple, and intelligent, she stepped naturally into the ingenuous parts (ingénuités). She attracted considerable attention in the little stage world, and Grétry, of the Opera Comique, seeing her and observing the proud humility with which she bore herself, referred to her always as "the little dethroned queen."

The little dethroned queen dwelt in a castle close against the sky, an apartment under the roof. Her only retainer was a humble dressing maid of the same theatre as herself, and her friend as well. She studied much and ate little. One day, after too long a fast, she was found in a faint at the foot of her stairway. Poor child, she was experiencing suffering in a way that refined her art, but left its blight forever on her life.

However, she was at that youthful age when even rags are becoming, and when the heart, in spite of its aching, will rejoice. She had her laughs as well as her cries. She and her poor companion, the dressing maid, living sparingly like two little birds, used to share their few crumbs with an occasional visitor. Once, when all the crumbs were gone, a big man with a very big appetite came to call. He talked eloquently of art, music, the drama, until he was tired, but no dinner appeared. At length, with the piteous gesture of a man faint for food, " Oh, my children," he cried. " No matter what! Anything! A large piece of bread! That surely cannot incommode you ! "

From Rouen to Brussels Mademoiselle Marceline travelled, to the Odéon, and back again to Brussels and Rouen. Her wandering habit, which was formed not of desire, but of necessity, began in this season of her theatrical career. She made

various débuts in the parts of " Julie " in the " Pot
de Fleurs " and " Eulalie " in " Misanthropy and
Repentance." At the Opera Comique she sang
with a thrilling, sympathetic voice. She was
especially successful in the pathetic parts. She
brought tears to many eyes, even to the eyes of a
certain malicious critic who went to ridicule and
remained to applaud.

She was also effective in the comic parts. But
these were an effort to her. It was difficult for
her to repress all feeling and to become merely a
pretty, smiling puppet. While she danced and
sang and performed her amusing little antics, she
lamented thus to herself:

> " In the vain shows where wit doth win applause,
> Hushed lies the heart and hidden :
> To please becomes the first of laws;
> To love is aye forbidden."

She began to weary of the " jester's crown," and
to desire, as she expressed it, " the sweet names of
wife and mother." In April, 1817, when she was
twenty years old, she married Monsieur Valmore,
who was of the same theatre as herself, and who
loved her deeply and ardently. For a few years
she and her husband acted together. Then she
retired from the stage.

Meanwhile she had lost her singing voice. But
she still heard the music in her brain. It was
" turning to poetry within her," Sainte Beuve ex-

plains. In 1817 she published her first volume of
verse. A second and third edition appeared in
1820 and 1822. They aroused interest and admiration. It was not until 1824–27, however, that
her reputation as a poet was established. From
that time on she wrote with increasing skill and
with a full development of her warm, sympathetic
genius. Sensibility was her domain. Her strains
were always sad and tender. "She had," said
Michelet, " the gift of tears, that gift which smites
the rock and dissipates the drought of the soul."
And Sophie Gay, quoting some of her verse, declared that it possessed the melancholy charm
which Monsieur de Ségur called the "luxury of
grief." There was nothing original, nothing start-
ling in the poetry of Madame Valmore. It was just
sweet and delicate and feminine, as frank and artless
as the poet who wrote it. In truth it was herself.

Madame Valmore and her poetry were one. But
her life, her exterior life that is, was very different.
It was a long wandering from lodging-house to
lodging-house, a hard fight for the necessities of
existence. A pension had been granted her. She,
sensitive and proud, had accepted it with extreme
reluctance. She spent much of it in charity, seeking always "to justify and purify" the money in
her eyes. The pension relieved the situation, but
after years of forced inactivity, when arrears had
accumulated into debts, total recovery was not
possible. The struggle still continued.

Madame Valmore noted with pain the effects of the struggle on herself and her family. " The rigors of fate too much prolonged," she said, " are as fatal to the mind as too much luxury. When it becomes necessary to work hard in order to escape absolute indigence, the wings of the soul are folded, and soaring is postponed to a future day."

Money difficulties were not Madame Valmore's only trouble. One by one she lost her dear ones, her brother, her sisters, her friends. At length death struck at her children, at little Inez grown to womanhood, and later at Undine, the beautiful and good and learned. Then in anguish she cried, " It is frightful, frightful to see the young die and to be left behind!" She felt lost, abandoned. For the first time her religion, her childlike faith, faltered. "I cannot always feel the angels sustaining me," she said.

But this was only for a moment. She, who was so afflicted, never despaired. The angels returned to her. She prayed to them as she prayed to God and the Virgin. Hers was an individual, an independent faith. She never attended service. She visited church only when it was empty. She desired no priest to intercede for her. She spoke direct to heaven. For this she was criticised. Yet no one was more intensely religious. She was always in the presence of God, Christ, the Virgin, and the dear departed. They were more real to her, more near to her than the affairs of the world.

Thus she lived close to Heaven, and caught somewhat the spirit of that neighborhood. She brought into her own atmosphere, so dingy and dusty and gray, a bit of the blue. What little money she had she shared with those who had less,—with her brother in the hospital at Douai and her sisters at Rouen, or some hungry actor or shivering poet. And when she had no money to bestow she was always ready with consoling words. She who had experienced so much suffering knew well how to compassionate the suffering of others. It was a theory of hers that the poor should help one another and ask no favors of the rich. "The rich cannot understand," she said. "Let us not speak of them except to rejoice that they do not suffer as we do." "Give until death," was her motto, and she gave freely and at all times of her purse, of her sympathy, and of her gift of song.

Meanwhile, she continued her wanderings, but found now and then in the midst of the desert an occasional oasis. Such was her visit to Milan. Her husband had been summoned thither as one of a troupe engaged to perform for the entertainment of the Emperor Ferdinand. Madame Valmore and her two daughters went with him. The engagement amounted to nothing, but the little family were afforded a glimpse of a romantic realm. The sunshine of the South brought a note of gladness to the sad voice of Madame Valmore. She sat beside her casement, whose only curtain was a verdant plane-tree, and with her family, "alone, in poor disguise," as she expressed it, she roamed "the grand Italian land." She breathed a warmth, she beheld a beauty that were free to all. Again, shortly after her journey to Italy and during the first of her residence in Paris, Madame Valmore visited Flanders with her husband. She enjoyed the merry Flemish holidays, and frequented the art galleries where black-robed virgins and portraits by Rubens and the head of the Laocoön filled her with an "inexpressible adoration."

On all such occasions Madame Valmore's heart responded ardently to the influence of culture and refinement. Her imagination was easily roused, her mind quickly diverted. "Oh," she exclaimed, "what a happy place this world is to one who possesses the faculty of admiration, at once the humblest and the proudest of all. It consoles one for all sorts of miseries, and gives wings to poverty, enabling it to soar above disdainful wealth!"

All that she needed, this woman of exquisite taste and sentiment, was a little space for reflection and study. Yet this was seldom granted. "I should have revelled in a study of the poets and poetry," she once said, "but have been fain to be content with dreaming of this as of the other good things of the world." And when at last the rare opportunity was offered and she was permitted to read, it was with an admiration so profound that she quite forgot herself, or if for a moment she remembered her own talent, it was to say, "The more I read the less I dare to write. I am smitten with terror. I am like a glow-worm in the sun."

She was very modest as to her own productions and grateful for honest criticism. Monsieur Latour, poet and professor, was her friend, and a literary adviser kind and affectionate. She appealed to him with characteristic humility, asking for light. He pointed out certain faults of expression, of carelessness and weakness, but found much to love and praise and pity in her verse. She thanked him, and by her sincerity, as she said, merited "that rarest of favors, truth."

Monsieur Latour was not the only denizen from the literary world who honored Madame Valmore with his friendship. There was also Lamartine, with whom she exchanged complimentary verses and letters; and Raspail, whom she hailed as "Dear Socrates," "Charming Stoic," and to whom she dedicated her pathetic plea, "Les Prisones et Les Prières;" and Brizeux, the Breton Virgil, of so strange, so flighty, so evanescent a character. Then, too, Béranger, Hugo, Vigny, Alexander Dumas, all paid their respects to her at one time or another. Though her star shone so obscurely and with so mild a light, it did not pass unseen, but was recognized and awarded its meed of appreciation and admiration.

Her husband, too, after long years of waiting and earnest endeavor, found his place at last. He

obtained, in September, 1852, honorable and congenial employment as editor of "The Catalogue"
in the Imperial Library. His appointment brought
"sacred content," it is said, to the members of the
humble household so perpetually and so sorely
tried.

Already there had been a slight lifting of the
clouds, a temporary period of cessation from suffering, of happiness and rejoicing. In January, 1851,
Undine was married. She went to the country, to
the estate of her husband, Monsieur Langlais,
at Saint Denis D'Anjon, and Madame Valmore
visited her there. Then, for the first time, this
mother and daughter enjoyed peace and freedom.
It was pleasant to live, they found, away from the
ringing of bells and literary and political wrangling. They rode on donkeys, they strayed pur-
poselessly through the meadows, they translated
Horace, they gathered fruits and flowers, they
breathed the scent of growing things and listened
to talk of the vintage, the wheat crop, and "hens
who lay continually." For the first time they experienced protracted sunshine and an easy life.

Yet, as the months passed, it became evident
that these benefits had come to Undine too late.
Madame Valmore regarded her child anxiously and
apprehensively. "Her countenance is so changeful," she wrote to Hippolyte. "She has so strange
an appetite and such a horror of walking. She is
so shy even in her confidences. It is as if her

heart were the home of thousands of birds who do not sing in concert, but fear and shun one another. She is always gentle, but so easily agitated."

It was the poison taking effect. The sunshine of a few months could not heal a weakness that was the result of the toil and privation of years. Her mother's watchful care, her husband's love, her baby's sweet dependence could not keep her. She died in February, 1853.

It was then that Madame Valmore entered the region of impenetrable shadows and became in very truth the " Mother of Sorrows." " I dare not write," she said, " for I cannot lie, and the tale is too sad to tell." Nevertheless, from out the darkness her voice still sounded submissive, clear, and undespairing, She had even yet at her command words of comfort and cheer. If she was the Mater Dolorosa of poetry, she was, to quote Raspail, its " good fairy," too. The tenth muse, he called her, the muse of virtue.

She who had always been so poor left, when she died, no fortune to her son. She could bequeath him only a name. Yet many fortunes, said one who knew her, might be given in exchange for such a patent of nobility.

Her tale, sad as the one she could not tell, has yet the breath of hope and consolation. It is a message, a word of wisdom, to all who suffer and must not despair.

MADAME DE RÉMUSAT.

Born at Paris, Jan. 5, 1780.
Died at Lille, Dec. 16, 1821.

" She was probably the woman (and consider what a blending of seriousness and grace this circumstance implies) with whom Napoleon and Talleyrand liked best to talk." — *Sainte Beuve.*

THE court was at Fontainebleau. There were gathered princes, electors, marshals, chamberlains, foreigners of distinction. Fear of the emperor and strict etiquette kept them cautious and restrained. One could not say that there was gaiety among them. Yet none of the symbols of gaiety were lacking. People danced, they played at chess and cards, they acted tragedies, they sang, they feasted, they hunted, they smiled, they laughed, they talked. Now and then, even, they abandoned themselves to a game of blind-man's-buff. They sought to assume the lightness and carelessness of children.

Among the illustrious personages who comprised this court was a woman who had attained a reputation for cleverness. She was known as Madame de Rémusat. Early in her court life she had spoken the name Shakspeare; she had defended the English author to Napoleon. Bonaparte had

269

turned upon her with a start. "Diable!" he had
exclaimed. "You are a savant!" The listening
audience had regarded her curiously. Thereafter
she had talked only idle talk or she had held her
tongue. Yet the name stuck. She was a "savant."
Madame herself was amused at her title. She
thought she had won her reputation rather too
easily.

She was not a beauty, this clever woman, but she
was attractive. A pen and ink portrait of the time,
done by an able hand, presents her to us. Her
figure, it is said, was good; her carriage graceful
and unaffected. Her features were not at all
remarkable, but her eyes, her lips, her teeth were
beautiful. Moreover, she was blessed with dimples. Her smile, therefore, was "sweet" and "arch."
Her face expressed "tenderness, vivacity, quick perception, a vivid imagination, and exquisite sensibility." Such, then, was Madame de Rémusat as
she appeared at court, Madame de Rémusat, Lady-
in-waiting to the Empress Josephine.

One evening Madame de Rémusat sat at the
piano in the palace of Fontainebleau playing Italian
dance music. The whole court passed before her.
She knew them all — knew them even to their
interests, their passions, their intrigues, and their
weaknesses. They seemed happy, free from
responsibility and anxiety. Yet, she meditated,
they had each in turn a favor to ask, justice to
demand, or some business of importance to trans-

act. They were behaving like children, while, in reality, their desires and their wills were those of men. They dared not show themselves. They were reduced to insignificance.

These thoughts were in her mind when, a moment later, the dance at an end, she rose from her seat at the piano. Talleyrand was at her side. The clever diplomat admired this clever woman and liked to find himself in her society. He spoke to her of some matter of importance in which he was intimately concerned. He spoke with his usual calm indifference. Madame de Rémusat regarded him a moment in silence. Then her thoughts demanding expression, and her face eloquent with her own earnestness, she exclaimed, "Mon Dieu, how is it possible that you can live and work without experiencing any emotion?"

He smiled upon her, and began to mock her as he mocked every one. "Ah, what a woman you are, and how young!" he observed.

Once this might have made her angry. Now his ridicule only amused her. She pitied more than she censured his hardness of heart. He had told her of his unfortunate youth, and she, who was so happy in her private life, was full of sympathy for him. Now and then, moreover, she had touched a chord in his nature, which told her that he had a soul, though it slept.

"Oh," she declared, "what a pity it is that you have to take such pains to spoil yourself. I can-

not help believing that the real *you* is better than
you are."

Later in the evening it was Napoleon who was
at Madame de Rémusat's side. He had recently restored lands and revenue to some Royalist friends
of hers, two young women whose father had been
a duke in the reign of Louis XVI. Madame
assured Bonaparte of their gratitude.

The emperor sneered. " Ouf ! " he declared.
" Gratitude ! That is a poetic word. It has no
meaning in the political world. These friends of
yours, who are grateful to me to-day, would rejoice
to-morrow if some Royalist should assassinate me."

Madame opened her eyes, surprised, incredulous.

Napoleon observed her expression. " You are
young," he said. " You don't know what party
hatred is. It is like a pair of spectacles — one sees
everybody, every opinion, every sentiment through
the glass of one's own passions."

Madame pondered a moment. She was one of
the few ladies of the court who comprehended the
conversation of the emperor and dared to answer
him in something more than monosyllables. " But,"
she demurred, " if you deny the existence of gratitude in your universe, for what reason do you
seek to win applause ? Why do you spend your
life in great and perilous enterprises ? "

" One cannot avoid one's destiny," he answered.
" He who is called cannot resist. Besides, human

pride finds the public it desires in the ideal world
which is called posterity."

Madame listened attentively. She was interested, but not convinced. She regarded the
emperor questioningly. "I shall never be able to
understand," she declared, "how a man can expose
himself to every sort of danger for posterity's sake
merely, while in his heart he despises the men of
his time."

At this Bonaparte spoke up quickly. "I do not
despise men, madame," he protested. "That is a
thing you must not say. I do not despise men, and
I particularly esteem the French."

At his abruptness Madame de Rémusat could
not repress a smile. It was as though, having forgotten himself a moment, he had expressed himself
too frankly, and suddenly bethought him of the
proper thing to say.

He saw the smile, guessed its meaning, and
answered it. He liked to be understood. He
drew near and pulled her ear. The act did not
surprise madame ; she knew it meant that he was
in a good humor — therefore, she did not draw
away, but received it like a courtier, smiling still.
"Mind, madame," he repeated, lifting a warning
finger, "you must never say that I despise the
French."

When next she was alone with her husband,
Madame de Rémusat drew a long sigh. Monsieur
de Rémusat asked her what it meant. Then she

expressed to him the feeling of oppression which all this cynicism gave her. Life at court was brilliant, but so unsatisfactory, she declared; there was no pleasure in it. She lifted her glance to her husband. Her dimples, showing, gave to her face that " sweet and arch " expression that so became her. " Indeed," she said, " the only pleasure I have ever found has been in our own home with you and mother and the boys."

This was Madame de Rémusat. She retained in the midst of scenes the most dazzling the simple tastes of her girlhood. When a woman of the world, experienced, influential, a social power, her chief interests were still domestic. Her mind reverted fondly to that pleasant Montmorency valley where leisure, seclusion, intellectual companionship and all the benefits of a happy home life had been hers.

She had gone first to that Montmorency valley a young girl, with her mother and her sister, when the Revolution issued its decree against the nobles and Paris was no longer habitable for them; for that lurid hue, which the Revolution cast on all surrounding objects, had colored Madame de Rémusat's early youth. Before it came, the little Claire, so she was called, was living peacably in Paris with her parents, Monsieur and Madame de Vergennes, and her younger sister Alix. Her father, Monsieur de Vergennes, was Master of Requests and later Director of the Vingtièmes, the tax on property.

He was nephew to that Comte de Vergennes who had been minister to Louis XVI. His family was an ancient one, aristocratic and illustrious. Madame de Vergennes, his wife, was a bright, practical, kindly woman of high principles and keenly vigorous mind. She superintended the education of her daughters. In that house in the Rue Saint Eustache where they lived, a large room was set apart as a school-room for the little girls. There their governess instructed them in book learning, and they were also taught the "frivolous arts,"— music, dancing, and drawing. Now and then, as they grew older, they were permitted occasional peeps at the big world. They were treated to a visit to the opera or a presentation at a ball.

At length the fateful year of '89 arrived. Monsieur de Vergennes took his place among the electors. Later he was made a member of the Council of the Commune and a mayor of the National Guard. He drifted resistlessly into the current of revolutionary madness. His wife, who was more prudent, more far-seeing, more prophetic than he, sought to restrain him. He listened to her when it was too late. He died on the scaffold in '94.

It was on the morrow of this tragedy in their home that Claire and her mother and little sister sought a refuge at Saint Gratien in the Montmorency valley, that fair land celebrated by Rousseau. Unprotected and in straightened circumstances, they were much in need of a devoted friend.

Such a friend they had in Augustin Laurent de
Rémusat.   This young man, at the outbreak of
the Revolution, had come to Paris as deputy from
Aix.   On his arrival in the city he had made the
acquaintance of Monsieur de Vergennes, and had
been a frequent visitor at the home of the Vergennes.   He had lived quietly and comparatively
unknown through those stormy years.   When the
widow de Vergennes and her two daughters emi-
grated, it was his wish to follow them.   His
services, his kindness, his loyal affection had
rendered him indispensable to the little family.
Madame de Vergennes could not oppose his wish.
He went with them to Saint Gratien.

One forms a pleasant picture of that family
circle at Saint Gratien.   There, the centre of the
group, was Madame de Vergennes, engaged in
some piece of sewing for one of her girls, now
relating a " piquant story," now " stimulating "
conversation by some interesting discussion, always
practical, cheerful, merry — an ideal mother.   Of
the two girls, Claire, who at the time of the migra-
tion to Montmorency was fourteen years of age, was
the more serious.   The little Alix was lively and
animated, much given to flights of fancy.   Claire
was a grave, studious maiden, very womanly for
her years, and something of a philosopher withal.
Monsieur de Rémusat was with them so constantly
that he, too, had come to be considered one of the
family.   Social, agreeable, courteous, he was a

delightful companion. He chatted with the mother;
he helped the daughters with their lessons. And,
more and more frequently, as the months went by
and he and Claire sat side by side at the round
table in the lamplight, the book of Horace lay
unnoticed between them. They spoke of other
things than Latin. Meanwhile, the eyes of Madame
de Vergennes rested contentedly upon them. She
did not anticipate, yet, when she saw the very
natural love which congeniality of tastes, intimacy,
solitude, and misfortune were engendering, she was
not surprised or sorry. She knew that her daughter's heart, though young, was ardent, sensitive,
emotional. She was glad to give it into the keeping of so good a man as Augustin de Rémusat.

Claire de Vergennes was married at the age of
sixteen to a man eighteen years her senior. He
was her director and instructor as well as husband.
There at Saint Gratien, in the same house
with Madame de Vergennes and Alix, Monsieur
de Rémusat and his young wife resided.
Their life after their marriage, as before, was quiet
and secluded, given to the pleasures of the country
and intellectual pursuits. Claire was a mother at
seventeen, and her education, as it has been phrased,
continued "under the tuition of her husband and
at the cradle of her son."

Not far from Saint Gratien, at Sannois, in that
same lovely Montmorency valley, lived Madame d'
Houdetot and her husband and Monsieur de Saint

Lambert. These were neighbors worth having. A friendly intercourse existed between the two households, and when Saint Gratien was sold, it was to Sannois that the Vergennes and the Rémusats removed. A way of communication was cut through the gardens of the two estates, and the ties of hospitality and friendship were even closer than before.

It was in the salon of Madame d' Houdetot that Madame de Rémusat was first introduced to fashionable and philosophic society. While Paris was yet in turmoil, peace reigned here, and the courtesies and amenities of life still flourished.

For Madame d' Houdetot herself, Madame de Rémusat entertained a sincere affection. She appreciated her charms, her talents, her cultivated tastes, and that benevolence and perennial youthfulness of mind which made Madame d' Houdetot so much beloved. And yet Madame de Rémusat was discreet in her affection. She recognized the danger of the elder woman's example. She recognized it, but it did not attract her. She spoke thus to her husband: " Madame d' Houdetot tells of past joys, of memories and regrets, with a sort of childishness and ignorance of evil, which seems to make her excusable. Any woman who was hesitating between love and virtue would do well to shun her; she is a hundred times more dangerous than an utterly corrupt person. She is so peaceful, so happy, so free from anxiety as to the next life. It would seem that she trusts to the words of the Gospel, ' Her sins, which are many, are forgiven; for she loved much.' Do not fear, however, that the sight of this tranquil old age following on an erring youth will upset my principles. I do not pretend to be stronger than others, but I feel that my virtue is secure because it is founded on happiness and love. I can be sure of myself because I love you and am beloved by you."

Another intimacy than this with Madame d' Houdetot, and one that was destined to prove more influential in the lives of the Rémusats, was that with Madame Bonaparte. She had been known to Madame de Vergennes as the widow of General Beauharnais, and later, at Malmaison, as the wife of that illustrious hero who was winning glory in the East. Madame Bonaparte, who always had need of confidants and who passionately desired sympathy, attached herself affectionately to Madame de Vergennes and her young daughters. Later, as the wife of the First Consul, Madame Bonaparte rose to a position of power. Meanwhile order had been restored in Paris. From the obscurity and poverty of their provincial home, the eyes of the young couple at Sannois turned wistfully to that field of opportunity and preferment. Then Madame Vergennes bethought her of her former friend, and applied to Madame Bonaparte for a position for her son-in-law. Madame Bonaparte received her graciously. She promised more than was expected, more even than was desired. In a very little while Monsieur de Rémusat was appointed Prefect of the Palace and Madame de Rémusat Lady-in-waiting to Madame Bonaparte. In their modesty Monsieur and Madame de Rémusat shrank from accepting such distinction, yet they dared not refuse. Truly it has been said that some have greatness thrust upon them.

At the time when Monsieur and Madame de Rémusat were drawn to the service of Napoleon, his court was just beginning. Its dignitaries were almost exclusively military. A name such as theirs, honorable and illustrious, and associated with the old régime, was one which the First Consul was proud to put upon his list. He showed them signal favor. In those early years he was at his best, young, natural, and as yet unspoiled by fortune. He charmed and dazzled Monsieur and Madame de Rémusat. Brought suddenly into the blaze of his glory, their eyes were blinded. They served him gladly, admiringly, unquestioningly. But later, as he became more and more confident, grew arrogant, and abused his power, they withdrew that absolute devotion. Little by little they were disillusioned. They found their hero not the hero they had thought him. It was the death of the Duke d' Engheim which began the work of disenchantment. That was a great grief to them. Madame could not speak of it for her tears. Thereafter their attitude was one of silent criticism. Napoleon felt their disaffection, and no longer showed them that marked attention which he had first awarded. Then their allegiance to the Empress Josephine, which continued unchanged after the divorce, removed them rather farther from his patronage. And, finally, their friendship for Talleyrand brought upon themselves a reflection of that minister's disgrace. They did not fall from favor, but they gradually ceased to be there.

For a long while, however, they were on the top wave. They formed a prominent and important part of a life that was overflowing with interest. They could not but be amused. Madame especially was entertained by the play going on about her. She was young,— twenty-two at the time of her appointment, — earnest, and enthusiastic. Things appealed to her imagination. She took an impersonal view of people and events ; she was interested in a disinterested way. Every evening she noted down the occurrences of the day. She compiled a valuable record which, alas, was not destined to survive its time.

This court life, its opportunities for conversation and experience, was a sort of literature to her — a book which she enjoyed reading. Of course her attitude was one which was sure to be misinterpreted. Ambitious people thought her ambitious. Selfish people accused her of intrigue. The unintelligent were a bit afraid of her; they could not forgive her for having opinions and views which they could not appreciate. She was pedantic they said. The name "savant," as applied to her, was spoken by others than the emperor. Nevertheless, Madame de Rémusat was a success. She was a woman of intelligence. She soon learned to adapt herself to her position. She acquired ease and address, and developed a talent for conversation. She was quick to perceive a thought; she listened well; she could follow a train of reasoning with understanding; she had the gift of the right word. It was for reasons such as these, no doubt, that Napoleon and Talleyrand liked to talk with her.

One can easily see that she was an excellent guide for Josephine Bonaparte. Despite her sweet and gracious disposition, the empress was jealous, frivolous, and flighty. She needed the support of a calm and prudent mind. Such support Madame de Rémusat could give. None knew this better than the emperor. Very often he was heard to say, " The empress is well advised."

The petty ambitions and dissensions of court life greatly amused Madame de Rémusat. One was joyous or one was depressed, accordingly as one was elevated to some new dignity or disregarded. All this seemed very absurd to Madame de Rémusat, but not at all surprising. One day she herself was in very good spirits, jesting with a company of friends. One of Bonaparte's aides-de-camp ac-

costed her. What new honor had been conferred
on her, he queried, curiously. Madame regarded
him a moment in bewilderment. Then, perceiving
his meaning, she laughed heartily. " Do you fancy,"
she retorted, " that at Saint Cloud one must always
be in tears if one is not a princess ? "

After the divorce and the empress's retirement
to Malmaison, the duties of Madame de Rémusat
were lightened. She was able to spend much of
her time in her own home. She was happy there,
and she was much visited. Among her frequent
guests were Monsieur Suard, the Abbé Morellet,
Monsieur Guizot, and she who afterwards became
Madame Guizot, that is Mademoiselle de Meulan,
Monsieur de Fontanes, Gérard, the painter, and
even, it has been whispered, Monsieur de Chateaubriand. Indeed, the drawing-room in her house, in
the Place Louis Quinz, legitimately takes its place
among the salons of the empire.

Later, under the Restoration, Monsieur de Rémusat was appointed Prefect of Toulouse and afterwards of Lille. Thus, in their middle life, as in
their early youth, Monsieur and Madame de Rémusat enjoyed together the pleasures of provincial
life, its retirement, its quiet, and its opportunities
for study and reflection. For Madame de Rémusat,
too, it afforded a chance to indulge her literary
talent.

For many years she had been an unsuspected
author. In her girlhood she wrote essays and

novelettes, and made metrical translations of the
" Odes of Horace." After her retirement from official life she wrote her " Memoirs of the Empire."
In her mind, and sometimes half confided to paper,
were numerous romances. Some of these she completed. Of these, " The Spanish Letters," begun
in 1804 at the Imperial Court and published in
1820, was the most important. It savored of her
court life; its characters suggested people of her
acquaintance; it had the touch, the tone of reality,
and, in addition, a vein of refined sentiment. Both
worldly and romantic, it was not unlike the author
herself. Madame de Rémusat's last literary labor
was her volume on the " Education of Women."
She looked into the future, to the new order that
was rising on the foundations of the old, and
pictured the ideal woman who, she hoped, might
come. She was a mother when she wrote, and her
interest was quickened by the thought that this
future which she contemplated would be the
present of her son.

And now we come to that fact in the career of
Madame de Rémusat which is, perhaps, its most
charming — that is her motherhood. In a brief
essay on " Coquetry," Madame de Rémusat expresses herself thus :

" It is in the years between thirty and forty
that women are commonly inclined to coquetry.
Younger, they please without effort, and by virtue
of their very ignorance. But when their spring-

time has passed, they begin to employ address in order to retain the homage which it would be painful to renounce. Sometimes they attempt to adorn themselves with a semblance of that innocence to which so much of their success is due. They are wrong. Every age has its advantages as well as its duties. A woman of thirty has seen the world, and has knowledge of evil, even if she has done nothing but good. At that age she is ordinarily a mother. At this crisis she must have the courage to unclasp the zone of Venus. Consider the charms whereof the poet declares it to be composed. Are they the ornaments of virtuous maternity?

> "'There Love, there young Desire,
> There fond Discourse, and there Persuasion dwelt,
> Which oft enthralls the mind of wisest man.'

"But what strength it requires to be the first to lay aside an ornament like this! With a little care, it would still so well become the wearer! Yet, a few more years, and the zone will fall of itself, refusing to deck charms that are already withered. Then how would one blush at the sight of it, sadly repeating like the Greek courtesan who consecrated her mirror to eternal beauty, 'I give thee to Venus, for she is always fair.'

"Is it not wise to provide in advance for our inevitable disappointment by anticipating it with courage? The sacrifices which reason dictates have this advantage,— that the effort they cost is in

itself their reward. Oh, mothers, gather your
children about you early. Dare to say when they
come into the world that your youth is passing into
theirs. Oh, mothers, be mothers, and you will be
wise and happy!"

When Madame de Rémusat wrote thus she was
thirty-two years old, an attractive woman still.
She might have kept her girdle longer without
impunity, and yet she has never been so fair, it
seems, than at this moment when she abandons it.
Nothing is wanting to her adornment, since she
wears so well that " majestic dignity " in praise of
which she speaks.

Madame de Rémusat was the mother of two
sons. Of Albert, the younger of the two, it has
been said: " His faculties never completely developed; he was a child to the end." To this son
she gave tender compassion and devoted care.
But it was Charles, the eldest, who satisfied her
hopes, who realized her ambitions, who filled her
heart. She was but seventeen years his senior;
their tastes, their feelings were delightfully congenial and intimate. They were not merely
mother and son, they were brother and sister, too.
She advised and encouraged him ; she put wise
thoughts into his head, the value of her experience.
In return he renewed her youth, for how could
she grow gray, in staid and emotionless maturity,
while she looked at the world through his ardent
young eyes?

It is pleasant to overhear this mother and son chatting confidentially together. They were the best of comrades, yet, on his part there was always filial reverence, and on hers maternal care.

"My dear boy," she writes to him at his school on the advent of his sixteenth birthday, "I follow you step by step in all your studies, and I see you are full of work during this month of July which I am passing so monotonously. I know pretty well, too, all you say and do on Thursdays and Sundays. Madame de Grasse tells me of your little talks, and amuses me with it all. For instance, she told me that the other day you had praised me to her, and said that when you and I talk together you are sometimes tempted to think me too clever. But you need not be checked by any fear of that, for you, my dear child, have at least as much wit as I. I tell you so frankly, because that gift, although an advantage, needs many other things to support it, and therefore you may take my words rather as warning than as praise. If my conversation with you often takes a serious turn, you must impute it to the fact that I am your mother, and have not relinquished that rôle. When I need no longer advise and warn you, we shall talk together quite at our ease, interchanging our reflections, our remarks, and our opinions on everything and everybody quite frankly, without fear of vexing each other; in fact, with all sincere and intimate friendship which, I believe, may perfectly well exist between a mother and a son. There are not so many years between us as to prevent me from sympathizing with your youth, or sharing some of your feelings. Women's shoulders wear young heads, and in the head of a mother one side is always just the same age as her child's.

"Madame de Grasse told me also that you want to amuse yourself during these holidays by writing some of your notions on various subjects. I think you are right. It will be interesting for you to read them again in a few years. Your father would say I want to make you a scribbler like myself, — for he does not stand on ceremony with me, — but I do not care. There can be no harm in setting down one's thoughts, in writing for one's own self alone, and I think both taste and style will be formed in this way."

Then she goes on to speak of still more intimate matters. She contemplates his character; she dwells especially on one point — his behavior to others.

"You are polite," she says, "more so, indeed, than is customary at your age; you have a pleasant manner in addressing people, and you are a good listener. Do not let this last quality slip. Madame de Sevigné says that appreciative silence is a mark of superior sense in young people. 'But, mother, what are you driving at? You promised to point out a fault, and hitherto I see nothing like one. A father's blow turns aside. Let us come to the fact, my dear mother.' So I will, my son, in a moment. I have a sore throat and can only speak slowly. Well, then, you are polite. When you are *asked* to do something which will gratify those you love, you consent willingly; but when an opportunity of so doing is merely pointed out to you, natural indolence and a certain love of self make you hesitate, and, when left to yourself, you do not seek such opportunities for fear of the trouble they may entail. Can you understand these subtle distinctions? While you are still partly under my authority I can influence and guide you, but you will soon have to answer for yourself, and I would wish you to think a little about other people, notwithstanding the claims of your own youth, which are naturally engrossing."

Thus did Madame de Rémusat perform the rôle of mother. She mixed praise and blame. She did not scold, she reasoned. She did not command, she pointed out the way. One cannot wonder that she endeared herself infinitely to her son, and, dying, bequeathed to him " a life-long sorrow."

The death of Madame de Rémusat occurred in 1821, when she was forty-one years of age. For her there was no decline. She died in the fulness of her powers. She was devoted to the welfare of her home, busy with her literary labors, inter-

ested in her husband's official career in the provinces, and in that literary success which her
talented son was already winning for himself in
Paris. She was still of the world, and in close
sympathy with it. And never had she been more
charming. She had grown easy, sprightly, merry,
with her years. She had brought earnestness into
society, and from society had derived freshness and
spontaneity.

Madame de Rémusat faced the mysterious beyond
with awe and trepidation. She reviewed her life.
Her charities had been trifling ; she had made few
sacrifices ; her life was almost empty of good
works. She was "puffed up" with her felicity;
proud of her titles of daughter, wife, and mother.
She had not hated, because her heart was full of
love. She had been virtuous, because she had been
happy. With such a record, how would God receive her? The Abbé Duval calmed her troubled
mind. Her happiness was a proof of God's love
he said. Religion very often demanded a life of
action. *She had served God in the world.* There
was her charity, her sacrifice, her work of piety.

It is a fitting encomium, this of the Abbé
Duval's. Let us take leave of Madame de Rémusat,
honoring her as he honored her, declaring with his
voice, "She served God in the world." No
epitaph could be found sweeter or more true.